Fresh Ways with
Vegetables

COVER
The warm tones of peppers and carrots contrast with the green of asparagus, mange-tout and French beans in a spring vegetable stir fry (recipe, page 80). Rapidly cooked in a minimum of hot oil, the vegetables have retained their vitamins and flavour as well as their fresh colours.

TIME-LIFE BOOKS

EUROPEAN EDITOR: Ellen Phillips
Design Director: Ed Skyner
Director of Editorial Resources: Samantha Hill
Chief Sub-Editor: Ilse Gray

Correspondents: Elisabeth Kraemer-Singh (Bonn); Dorothy Bacon (London); Maria Vincenza Aloisi, Josephine du Brusle (Paris); Ann Natanson (Rome).

LOST CIVILIZATIONS
HOW THINGS WORK
SYSTEM EARTH
LIBRARY OF CURIOUS AND UNUSUAL FACTS
BUILDING BLOCKS
A CHILD'S FIRST LIBRARY OF LEARNING
VOYAGE THROUGH THE UNIVERSE
THE THIRD REICH
MYSTERIES OF THE UNKNOWN
TIME-LIFE HISTORY OF THE WORLD
FITNESS, HEALTH AND NUTRITION
HEALTHY HOME COOKING
UNDERSTANDING COMPUTERS
THE ENCHANTED WORLD
LIBRARY OF NATIONS
PLANET EARTH
THE GOOD COOK
THE WORLD'S WILD PLACES

New edition © 1995 Time-Life Books Inc. All rights reserved.
This edition published 1995 by Brockhampton Press, a member of Hodder Headline PLC.
First published 1986 by Time-Life Books Inc,

No part of this book may be reproduced in any form or by any electronic or mechanical means, including information storage and retrieval devices or systems, without prior written permission from the publisher, except that brief passages may be quoted for review.

ISBN 1 86019 076 6
TIME-LIFE is a trademark of Time Warner Inc. U.S.A.

HEALTHY HOME COOKING

SERIES DIRECTOR: Dale M. Brown
Deputy Editor: Barbara Fleming
Series Administrator: Elise Ritter Gibson
Designer: Herbert H. Quarmby
Picture Editor: Sally Collins
Photographer: Renée Comet
Text Editor: Allan Fallow
Editorial Assistant: Rebecca C. Christoffersen

Editorial Staff for *Fresh Ways with Vegetables:*
Book Manager: Andrea E. Reynolds
Writer: Margery A. duMond
Researcher/Writers: Scarlet Cheng (photography), Jean Getlein, Susan Stuck
Copy Co-ordinators: Marfé Ferguson, Elizabeth Graham
Picture Co-ordinator: Linda Yates

Special Contributors: Carol Gvozdich (nutrition analysis), Nancy Lendved (props), Ann Ready (charts)

European Edition:
Designer: Lynne Brown
Sub-Editor: Wendy Gibbons
Production Co-ordinator: Nikki Allen
Production Assistant: Maureen Kelly

THE COOKS

ADAM DE VITO began his cooking apprenticeship when he was only 14. He has worked at Le Pavillon restaurant, in Washington, D.C., taught with cookery author Madeleine Kamman, and conducted classes at L'Académie de Cuisine in Maryland.

HENRY GROSSI was awarded a Grand Diplôme at the École de Cuisine La Varenne in Paris. He then served as the school's assistant director and as its North American business and publications co-ordinator.

JOHN T. SHAFFER is a graduate of The Culinary Institute of America at Hyde Park, New York. He has had broad experience as a chef, including five years at The Four Seasons Hotel in Washington, D.C.

CONSULTANTS

CAROL CUTLER is the author of many cookery books. During the 12 years she lived in France, she studied at the Cordon Bleu and the École des Trois Gourmandes, as well as with private chefs. She is a member of the Cercle des Gourmettes and a charter member and past president of Les Dames d'Escoffier.

NORMA MACMILLAN has written several cookery books and edited many others. She has worked on various cookery publications, including *Grand Diplôme* and *Supercook*. She lives and works in London.

NUTRITION CONSULTANTS

JANET TENNEY has been involved in nutrition and consumer affairs since she received her master's degree in human nutrition from Columbia University. She is the manager for developing and implementing nutritional programmes for a major chain of supermarkets in the Washington, D.C., area.

PATRICIA JUDD trained as a dietician and worked in hospital practice before returning to university to obtain her MSc and PhD degrees. For the last 10 years she has lectured in Nutrition and Dietetics at London University.

SPECIAL CONSULTANT

SANDRA CONRAD STRAUSS, the former vice president of consumer affairs for the United Fresh Fruit and Vegetable Association, is president of Consumer Concepts, Oakton, Virginia, a consulting firm specializing in consumer education about fresh produce. She is the author of *Fancy Fruits and Extraordinary Vegetables* a cookery book that features some of the most unfamiliar and unusual produce items available in supermarkets today.

This volume is one of a series of illustrated cookery books that emphasize the preparation of healthy dishes for today's weight-conscious, nutrition-minded eaters.

Fresh Ways with Vegetables

BY

THE EDITORS OF TIME-LIFE BOOKS

BROCKHAMPTON PRESS

Contents

Baked Asparagus with Pine-Nuts and Gruyère

Stuffed Mushrooms with Goat Cheese and Spinach

3 *A Fruitful Abundance* 57

Kale Calzones

Honey-Glazed Shallots with Mint

4 Down-to-Earth Delights 87

Sherry-Glazed Turnips

5 Microwaving for Flavour and Health 119

Stir-Fried Vegetables with Sesame Seeds

Vegetables' Varied Riches

What would good eating be without the colour, variety and flavour provided by fresh vegetables? And what would good health be without the vitamins and minerals they so abundantly offer? Indeed, vegetables contribute as much as 50 per cent of the vitamin C and 25 per cent of the vitamin A consumed in food by the average person in one year. Consisting of 70 to 95 per cent water, with almost no fat or oil, vegetables have so few calories that most can be eaten without concern for weight gain. And were this not enough to recommend vegetables to lovers of fine cooking who wish to eat well without doing harm to themselves, vegetables are also blessedly free of cholesterol and generally very low in sodium.

At the same time, they are a source of dietary fibre, which aids digestion and may lower the level of blood cholesterol. Moreover, some vegetables, such as potatoes, peas, sweetcorn and winter squash, are particularly high in carbohydrates, which the body needs for energy, especially now, as people try to cut down on fats in their diets. The good news, of course, is that carbohydrates have about half as many calories weight for weight as fat.

Even more exciting is the possibility that vegetables, as well as fruits and whole-grain cereal products, may help to reduce the risk of cancer, particularly of the gastrointestinal tract. While this has yet to be proved, studies involving animals and people suggest that fibre, some vitamins and certain other substances present in these foods inhibit the disease.

A growing taste for vegetables

More than 200 kinds of vegetables are relished around the world; this book treats 66 of them. Most of these are commonly available, but there are others that only recently have begun to enjoy wider distribution, reflecting a trend by the retail trade to broaden their selection of fresh produce in response to both a growing sophistication among customers and the rapidly developing interest in nutrition. The number of vegetables displayed on the shelves has more than doubled in the last decade or so as the per capita consumption of fresh vegetables has risen to over 100 kg (200 lb) a year in the U.K.

Such exotics as the chayote, or christophine (a lime green, deeply furrowed squash), the okra (a small green pod also called lady's finger because of its elegantly tapering shape), and the shiitake mushroom with its pungent wild flavour, are only three of the many "new" vegetables that are bringing excitement to cooking. As travel becomes ever easier, and populations more multi-cultural, the demand for ethnic foods has increased.

Some vegetables, fortunately, are being rediscovered. The sweet potato, for example, though well-known to Americans, has only recently made its appearance on European supermarket shelves; yet it was very popular in Elizabethan England. Originally introduced to Europe by Columbus in the 15th century, it was later given a culinary revival by Napoleon's Josephine.

The Jerusalem artichoke, brought to Europe from North America by 17th-century explorers, is also making a comeback. Thanks to its slightly sweet flavour and its crunchy texture, it has found a place in the new, lighter cooking. Beet greens, once tossed aside by all but farmers' wives, who knew a good thing when they saw one, are beginning to receive the attention they deserve from imaginative cooks. Even the common cabbage has begun to regain some of its old popularity in inventive dishes that bring out its special flavour. What is more, it is now widely available in several delicious varieties, including the hitherto little-known bok choy and the Chinese cabbage, once found only in Asian markets. They are well worth trying, as are all the other less familiar vegetables featured in this cookery book.

Needless to say, vegetables taste best when picked fresh, cooked immediately and brought promptly to the table. There can be no greater pleasure than sweetcorn served and eaten within minutes of harvesting. More and more people have taken to growing their own vegetables in kitchen gardens to guarantee themselves a ready supply, and every year the mail order seed catalogues offer a wider range of new and unusual species; others buy in local markets; but most cooks still rely on shops and supermarkets for their produce. The quality can, of course, be very good, especially if the vegetables have been properly transported and handled to ensure that they retain as much of their flavour and as many of their nutrients as possible. But if they have been unnecessarily exposed to light and held at room temperature for even one day, most of them will have deteriorated nutritionally. Green beans, for example, lose half their vitamin C when left unrefrigerated for 24 hours.

Selecting the finest

In shopping for vegetables, pick those that are bright in colour and crisp or firm in texture. The healthy-looking carrot, with its deep orange colour, will contain several times more carotene — which is converted to vitamin A in the body — than the limp, pale one. Indeed, the deeper the orange, yellow or green of a vegetable, the higher its potential for supplying vitamin A will be. When it comes to root and stem vegetables, select the smaller ones; the bigger, older specimens are likely to contain a higher percentage of lignin, a tough, woody material that does not soften during cooking. Reject bruised and blemished vegetables, and any that have cracks or tears or have been chewed by insects; such damage makes it easy for bacteria to enter the tissue.

After purchase, such perishable vegetables as leafy greens should not be washed until you are ready to use them; this will minimize vitamin and mineral loss and curtail the growth of bacteria. But if the vegetables are dirty and need to be rinsed, shake them well, wrap them in paper towels to absorb any excess moisture, and then place the vegetables in plastic bags or in other closable containers before putting them in the refrigerator.

Generally speaking, vegetables that easily wilt or dry out should be kept in a dark, cool and slightly humid atmosphere. This restricts the proliferation of bacteria and mould, prevents dehydration and suppresses enzymes in the vegetables that, once they are activated, lead to loss of flavour and texture, and ultimately to decay. Spinach, broccoli and celery are only three of many vulnerable vegetables that will maintain their quality longer if they are refrigerated at around 2° to 5°C (35° to 40°F) and at high humidity. The vegetable crisper, the refrigerator's bottom drawer, is a perfect environment for them.

Among the hardier vegetables that need not — in fact, should not — be refrigerated are potatoes (cold converts their starch to sugar), sweet potatoes, onions and winter squash. All require cool, dark, well-ventilated conditions. The household root cellar of old, with its 10° to 13°C (50° to 55°F) temperature, was based on sound wisdom; it prevented the potatoes and other vegetables stored there from sprouting, withering or rotting. A cupboard on an outside wall, away from the stove or refrigerator, or a cool, airy basement provides a modern substitute.

When it comes to preparing and cooking them, vegetables require care; they are, after all, living things that continue to respire, or "breathe", after leaving the farm (asparagus actually continues to grow). If you did not wash the vegetables before storing them, rinse them under running water; scrub tough-skinned vegetables with a vegetable brush. Trim sparingly; the green outer leaves of cabbage, for example, are high in food value, and unless they are tough or wilted, these leaves are well worth eating. Peel thinly wherever possible. As opposed to a paring knife, which cuts deeper, a peeler with a so-called floating blade removes only the top layer, leaving the nutrients directly beneath the skin intact. Whenever you can keep vegetables' skins on, do so; not only are they a good source of fibre, they also contain vitamins and minerals.

Slice or chop with a sharp knife, and when slicing, use a sawing motion; this will reduce bruising of surfaces and further save nutrients. Avoid soaking sliced, chopped or peeled vegetables; soaking leaches out minerals and water-soluble vitamins, especially if the pieces are small. And try not to leave the vegetables exposed to air and light. Cook them as soon as you can.

Cooking to preserve nutrients

All good cooks want the food they prepare to be delicious; fortunately, the methods and techniques most often recommended by nutritionists for cooking fresh vegetables guarantee flavour as well as preserve nutrients. Generally speaking, vegetables need to be cooked only until they are tender but still slightly crisp.

The most misunderstood cooking method, alas, is the one most commonly employed: boiling. When a lot of water is used and the process is prolonged, boiling can destroy as much as 80 per cent of a vegetable's vitamin C, and cook and leach out other vitamins and various minerals as well. Too many well-meaning people throw away far more nourishment than they realize when they pour the cooking water down the drain; an experiment conducted by the U.S. Army showed that the water in which cabbage had been boiled contained more B vitamins than the vegetable itself. Providing it is not bitter or unattractive in colour, the cooking liquid can be used profitably in stock, sauce or soup.

To conserve nutrients and enhance flavour, most vegetables benefit from being cooked in only enough water to cover them. Be sure that the water is boiling before you plunge your vegetables into it. Then let the water come back to the boil, cover the saucepan, and reduce the heat to achieve a slow boil. By putting the lid on, you trap the steam and hasten the cooking process. Bear in mind, however, that after 5 to 7 minutes with the lid on, green vegetables will lose much of their colour, and that the flavour of vegetables with a high sulphur content, such as cabbage and cauliflower, will intensify, along with their odour. Green vegetables suffer because the acids they contain are released into the water and convert the bright

The Key to Better Eating

This book, like others in the Healthy Home Cooking series, presents an analysis of nutrients contained in a single serving of each dish, listed beside the recipe itself, as on the right. Approximate counts for calories, protein, cholesterol, total fat, saturated fat (the kind that increases the body's blood cholesterol) and sodium are given.

Healthy Home Cooking addresses the concerns of today's weight-conscious, health-minded cooks by providing recipes that take into account guidelines set by nutritionists. The secret of eating well, of course, has to do with maintaining a balance of foods in the diet; most of us consume too much sugar and salt, too much fat and too many calories, even too much protein. In planning a meal, the cook using the recipes in this book should take into account what the rest of the meal is likely to contribute nutritionally. The cook should also bear in mind that moderation, as in all things, is a good policy to follow when seeking to prepare a balanced meal.

Interpreting the chart

The chart below gives dietary guidelines for healthy men, women and children. Recommended figures vary from country to country, but the principles are the same everywhere. Here, the average daily amounts of calories and protein are from a report by the U.K. Department of Health and Social Security; the maximum advisable daily intake of fat is based on guidelines given by the National Advisory Committee on Nutrition Education (NACNE); those for cholesterol and sodium are based on upper limits suggested by the World Health Organization.

The volumes in the Healthy Home Cooking series do not purport to be diet books, nor do they focus on health foods. Rather, they express a commonsense approach to cooking that uses salt, sugar, cream, butter and oil in moderation while employing other ingredients that also provide flavour and satisfaction. Herbs, spices, aromatic vegetables, fruits, wines and vinegars are all used towards this end.

Calories **110**
Protein **5g**
Cholesterol **5mg**
Total fat **4g**
Saturated fat **0g**
Sodium **130mg**

The recipes make few unusual demands. Naturally they call for fresh ingredients, offering substitutes when these are unavailable. (The substitute is not calculated in the nutrient analysis, however.) Most of the ingredients can be found in any well-stocked supermarket; the occasional exception can be bought in speciality or ethnic shops.

In Healthy Home Cooking's test kitchens, heavy-bottomed pots and pans are used to guard against foods burning and sticking whenever a small amount of oil is used; non-stick pans are utilized as well. Both safflower oil and virgin olive oil are favoured for sautéing. Safflower was chosen because it is the most highly polyunsaturated vegetable fat available in supermarkets, and polyunsaturated fats reduce blood cholesterol; if unobtainable, use sunflower oil, also high in polyunsaturated fats. Virgin olive oil is used because it has a fine fruity flavour lacking in the lesser grade known as "pure". In addition, it is — like all olive oil — high in monounsaturated fats, which are thought not to increase blood cholesterol. Sometimes both virgin and safflower oils are combined, with olive oil contributing its fruitiness to the safflower oil. When virgin olive oil is unavailable, "pure" may be substituted.

About cooking times

To help the cook plan ahead effectively, Healthy Home Cooking takes time into account in all of its recipes. While recognizing that everyone cooks at a different speed, and that stoves and ovens differ in temperatures, the series provides approximate "working" and "total" times for every dish. Working time stands for the minutes actively spent on preparation; total time includes unattended cooking time, as well as any other time devoted to marinating, steeping or soaking various ingredients. Since the recipes emphasize fresh foods, they may take a bit longer to prepare than quick and easy dishes that call for canned or packaged products, but the payoff in flavour and often in nutrition should compensate for the little extra time involved.

Recommended Dietary Guidelines

		Average Daily Intake		Maximum Daily Intake			
		CALORIES	PROTEIN grams	CHOLESTEROL milligrams	TOTAL FAT grams	SATURATED FAT grams	SODIUM milligrams
Females	7-8	1900	47	300	80	32	2000*
	9-11	2050	51	300	77	35	2000
	12-17	2150	53	300	81	36	2000
	18-54	2150	54	300	81	36	2000
	54-74	1900	47	300	72	32	2000
Males	7-8	1980	49	300	80	33	2000
	9-11	2280	57	300	77	38	2000
	12-14	2640	66	300	99	44	2000
	15-17	2880	72	300	108	48	2000
	18-34	2900	72	300	109	48	2000
	35-64	2750	69	300	104	35	2000
	65-74	2400	60	300	91	40	2000

*(or 5g salt)

green chlorophyll initially revealed by the cooking process into dull olive. Vegetables containing sulphur become malodorous as sulphides multiply during the cooking. In a trade-off, the cook might wish to use more water to dilute the acids and leave the lid off the pan so that the volatile acids and the sulphides that may also be present can escape with the steam, but cooking will take longer and some of the nutrients will be lost. Critical here, then, is the cooking time — the shorter, the better.

Where nutrition is concerned, steaming is a sounder method of cooking than boiling. This is because the vegetables cook in the water vapour rather than in the water itself. Steamed broccoli, for example, retains almost 80 per cent of its vitamin C — boiled broccoli only 33 per cent. The colour is also better; the volatile acids in the vegetables rise with the steam to the lid and then run down the sides of the pan into the water below, and thus do not have any sustained contact with the vegetables. To ensure that the vegetables will cook evenly, distribute them loosely in the steamer; this allows the vapour to circulate round them. And since those at the bottom can overcook, it pays to use a steamer large enough to spread the vegetables out evenly. A metal vegetable steamer or steaming basket is a good investment — but a steamer can easily be improvised from a colander or a strainer positioned over a saucepan with a tightly fitting lid. Add the vegetables to the steamer only after the water is boiling; the high temperature helps to inactivate enzymes that would otherwise destroy the vitamin C.

Some steaming can be done without a steamer at all. A leafy vegetable such as spinach — which has a high moisture content to begin with — will have enough water clinging to it after rinsing to allow the vegetable to be steamed in a covered saucepan without additional water. With a tougher leafy vegetable like spring greens, a couple of tablespoons of water will effectively aid the cooking process.

Sautéing and stir-frying are two other nutritionally sound methods. The trick is to cut or slice the vegetables small or thin enough so that the heat can penetrate them quickly, and to use the smallest amount of oil possible (only a tablespoon or so will do) so as not to elevate the calorie count unduly. Stirred and tossed over high heat in the few minutes required to cook most vegetables by the sauté or stir-fry method, they surrender little of their nutritional value. In addition, sautéed or stir-fried vegetables keep much of their colour, which further enhances their appeal. Sautéing and stir-frying are suitable for almost all vegetables; when several are to be combined in a dish, first cook those that need more time, then add those requiring less.

Baking and braising have advantages of their own. Whether topped by a lid or a protective coating of crumbs or cheese, the vegetables cook in their own juices. Braising done in a small amount of liquid is nutritionally beneficial when the liquid is consumed with the vegetable. Braising is particularly effective carried out over low heat. Grilling, involving high heat, destroys some nutrients. And because oil or fat must be used to keep the vegetables from becoming dry, the calorie count inevitably goes up. Still, it may be exactly the right method for some recipes. As in all such matters, common sense should prevail.

For cooks who have microwave ovens, a whole new horizon opens up for vegetables. Microwaving preserves not only colour but nutrients as well. And there is the further advantage of speed (recipes, pages 119-130).

Some special considerations

Whatever the cooking method, freshly cooked vegetables should be served promptly — not kept warm in an oven or set aside and reheated. Nor, once they have been cooked, should they be stored long in the refrigerator; after only a day's refrigeration, they will have lost a quarter of their vitamin C, and each new day will bring a further loss. (A good use for many leftover vegetables is in a salad.) While garden vegetables may be profitably frozen for subsequent cooking, fresh vegetables that are cooked and then frozen, later to be thawed and reheated, will be not only unpleasantly mushy but less nutritious as well.

The dishes in this book are organized by type of vegetable. The first section deals with shoots, stems and flowers, which is not the exotic collection it may at first seem, but a set of mouth-watering recipes for asparagus, fennel and broccoli, among others. The second section is devoted to leafy vegetables. The third includes pods, fruit vegetables and seeds — everything from mange-tout to sweet peppers to broad beans. The fourth consists of recipes for such roots, tubers and bulbs as carrots, potatoes and onions. The final section is devoted to cooking vegetables in the microwave oven. At the end of the book a chart presents basic nutritional information pertaining to the vegetables found in the recipes; a second chart gives tips on buying and storing them. Since unsalted chicken stock is an ingredient in many of the dishes, a recipe for it appears on page 139, along with one for a meatless vegetable stock that may be used instead.

Scattered throughout the recipes are various members of the mustard, cabbage and turnip families, the so-called cruciferous vegetables. Among these are cauliflower, broccoli, Brussels sprouts, kohlrabi, swedes, kale and spring greens. A mere 100 g (3 oz) of cooked broccoli provides 120 per cent of the Recommended Daily Amount of vitamin C, 50 per cent of the RDA of vitamin A and thiamine, and close to one tenth of the RDA of calcium and iron. Recent scientific research has revealed that of the vegetables covered in this book, the crucifers may be the most important in lowering the risk of certain cancers, suggesting that mothers were right all along — vegetables are good for you.

1 Steamed broccoli clad in a red pepper sauce (recipe, page 27) stands among ceramic, china and paper renditions of the vegetables featured in this section.

An Edible Bouquet

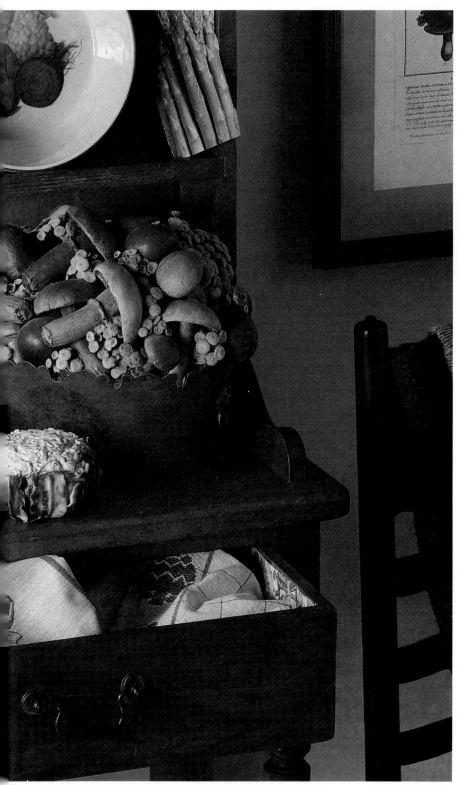

Many more of us eat flowers than we might suppose. Broccoli, cauliflower and artichokes are nothing more than immature blossoms. If an artichoke were allowed to bloom, it would look like a thistle which, in fact, it is. The green leaves we relish are the flower's bracts and the bottom is its base, while the fuzzy choke is the undeveloped purple head of the thistle. Anyone who has kept broccoli too long knows that the florets turn yellow as their myriad buds open. So will the flower clusters of the cauliflower.

In addition to the edible flowers, this section includes shoots, stems and sprouts as varied as asparagus, bulb fennel, bok choy and kohlrabi. These may be prepared singly or combined with other vegetables, and can be enhanced by light sauces or dressings.

Some vegetables in the section require special handling. Artichokes, for example, will discolour when their cut surfaces are exposed to air, and also during the cooking process, unless preventive steps are taken. Rubbing the surfaces with lemon or lime juice and adding lemon or lime to the cooking water guards against this. Cooking the artichokes in a non-reactive pan — such as an enamelled or stainless steel saucepan — prevents chemical reaction that would further discolour them. Instructions for preparing whole artichokes, as well as for artichoke bottoms, appear on pages 12 and 13.

Asparagus spears need only to have their tough woody bottoms snapped off to be delicious, but lightly peeling them as well ensures optimum tenderness. Swiss chard — really two vegetables in one — has both stems and leaves to offer the cook. The stems can be trimmed from the leaves with scissors or a knife. If only the stems are used, the greens can be reserved for another meal. Bok choy, or Chinese chard, now more widely available thanks to a new method of planting, can also do double duty in this way.

Anyone in an adventurous mood who does not already know and like kohlrabi should try this plump, light-green or lavender stem vegetable that looks like a bulb but grows above ground as an enlarged part of the stem. Its name means "cabbage turnip" in German, and it is not unlike both in flavour. Bulb, or Florence, fennel is another stem vegetable deserving wider appreciation. Its liquorice, or anise, flavour contributes a subtle note to dishes. As sophisticated a diner as American President Thomas Jefferson grew bulb fennel in his garden at Monticello, Virginia, on the enthusiastic recommendation of a friend who sent him the seeds from Italy. "The fennel," wrote the friend, "is beyond every other vegetable, Delicious."

and continue cooking for 2 minutes, stirring frequently. Add the chopped garlic, basil and tomatoes, and 12.5 cl (4 fl oz) of the stock. Bring the mixture to the boil, then reduce the heat and simmer for 10 minutes. Remove the saucepan from the heat.

In a heavy, 4 litre (7 pint) saucepan or a fireproof casserole with a lid, melt the remaining butter over medium-low heat. Add the rice and cook, stirring constantly, until the rice is opaque — 3 to 4 minutes. Stir in the vegetable mixture, ¼ litre (8 fl oz) of the stock and the pepper, and bring to the boil. Reduce the heat and simmer, covered, for 10 minutes.

Gently stir in the artichoke bottoms, the remaining stock and the Parmesan cheese, and continue to cook the dish, covered, until the rice is tender and the liquid is absorbed — 10 to 15 minutes.

Garnish with the parsley; serve immediately.

Artichoke Bottoms with Tomato and Rice

Serves 8
Working time: about 25 minutes
Total time: about 45 minutes

Calories **205**
Protein **6g**
Cholesterol **15mg**
Total fat **9g**
Saturated fat **4g**
Sodium **190mg**

4	artichoke bottoms (page 13)	4
½	lemon	½
40 g	unsalted butter	1¼ oz
2 tbsp	virgin olive oil	2 tbsp
125 g	mushrooms, wiped clean and sliced	4 oz
¼ tsp	salt	¼ tsp
1	small onion, finely chopped	1
1	garlic clove, finely chopped	1
2 tsp	chopped fresh basil, or ¾ tsp dried basil	2 tsp
2	tomatoes, skinned, seeded (page 84) and chopped	2
½ litre	unsalted chicken or vegetable stock	16 fl oz
175 g	rice	6 oz
	freshly ground black pepper	
60 g	Parmesan cheese, freshly grated	2 oz
10 g	parsley, chopped	⅓ oz

In a large, non-reactive saucepan, bring 1 litre (1¾ pints) of water to the boil. Squeeze the juice of the lemon into the water and add the lemon itself. Cook the artichoke bottoms in the boiling water for 10 minutes. Drain them and cut each into six wedges.

In a small, heavy-bottomed saucepan, heat 15 g (½ oz) of the butter with the olive oil over medium heat. Add the mushrooms and salt, and sauté until the liquid from the mushrooms has evaporated. Stir in the onion

Cooking Artichokes

Though artichokes are often cooked by immersing them in lots of boiling water, steaming them in just a little retains more of their nutrients and flavour. A microwave oven abbreviates the cooking time and preserves even more nutrients. For either method, wash the artichokes and prepare them beforehand as shown opposite, above.

To steam artichokes, pour enough water into a large, non-reactive pan to fill it about 2.5 cm (1 inch) deep; add 2 tablespoons of lemon juice and stand the artichokes upright in the water. Cover the pan and bring the water to the boil, then reduce the heat to medium low. After 25 minutes, test the artichokes: a knife tip inserted in an artichoke bottom should meet no resistance, and a leaf gently tugged should easily pull free. Any artichoke that fails these tests should be cooked 5 minutes more and re-tested. At the end of the steaming process, remove the artichokes from the pan and stand them upside down to drain.

To microwave artichokes, wrap them individually in plastic film, making sure that water from the washing still clings to their leaves. Pierce the film. Place each one upside down in a glass ramekin in the microwave oven and cook them on high. For a single artichoke, allow 4 to 7 minutes' cooking time; for each additional artichoke in the batch, add approximately 3 minutes more. Half way through the cooking time, rotate each ramekin 180 degrees to ensure even cooking. Let the cooked artichokes stand, still wrapped, for 5 minutes before serving them.

Preparing a Whole Artichoke for Cooking

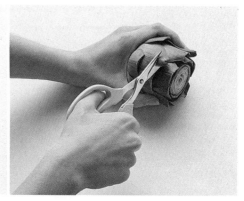

1 *TRIMMING THE TOP. With a stainless steel knife, cut off about 2.5 cm (1 inch) of the top (above). To prevent discoloration, immediately rub the cut edges with a juicy, freshly cut lemon.*

2 *REMOVING THE STEM. Cut off the stem at the base of the globe so that the artichoke will sit upright when served. (Some people prefer to snap off the stem.) Remove the ring of small or discoloured leaves at the base and discard them.*

3 *SNIPPING THE LEAF TIPS. With a pair of kitchen scissors, trim off the hard, prickly tips of the exposed whole leaves. The artichoke is now ready for cooking (instructions, page 12).*

Preparing an Artichoke Bottom

1 *REMOVING THE OUTER LEAVES. Remove two or three outer layers of artichoke leaves by pulling each leaf out and down until it snaps off at its base. Stop when you reach the tender, yellow-green inner leaves of the artichoke.*

2 *CUTTING OFF THE TOP. Holding a stainless-steel knife about 4 cm (1½ inches) above the rounded base of the artichoke, slice straight down to remove the top. Discard the top.*

3 *REMOVING THE STEM. With a single, even stroke, cut off the stem of the artichoke flush with the rounded base. (Alternatively, it can be snapped off.) Discard the stem and rub the base of the artichoke with cut lemon.*

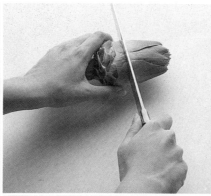

4 *PARING THE BOTTOM. Turn the artichoke base up. Slowly rotating the vegetable with one hand, use a paring knife held at an angle to cut off the dark green bases of the leaves. Moisten the cut surfaces with lemon.*

5 *TRIMMING THE ARTICHOKE. Turn the artichoke over. With the same spiral cutting motion you used to pare the bottom, trim off the light green parts from the upper half of the artichoke. Rub the cut surfaces with lemon.*

6 *REMOVING THE CHOKE. With a sturdy teaspoon, scrape out the choke — the densely packed, hairy centre of the artichoke — and discard it. What remains is the bottom. Drop the bottom into acidulated water to preserve its colour.*

Red Pepper and Tomato Sauce for Artichokes

Serves 4
Working time: about 30 minutes
Total time: about 1 hour and 30 minutes

Calories **195**
Protein **4g**
Cholesterol **0mg**
Total fat **14g**
Saturated fat **1g**
Sodium **170mg**

4	artichokes, trimmed, cooked (pages 12 and 13) and chilled	4
1	large sweet red pepper	1
2½ tbsp	safflower oil	2½ tbsp
1½ tbsp	virgin olive oil	1½ tbsp
2	ripe tomatoes, skinned, seeded (page 84) and coarsely chopped	2
1 tsp	tomato paste (optional)	1 tsp
1 tbsp	chopped shallot	1 tbsp
1	garlic clove, finely chopped	1
2 tbsp	chopped fresh basil, or 2 tsp dried basil	2 tbsp
1	spring onion, trimmed and chopped	1
2 tbsp	balsamic vinegar, or 1½ tbsp red wine vinegar mixed with ½ tsp honey	2 tbsp
¼ tsp	salt	¼ tsp
	freshly ground black pepper	

Peel the red pepper with a vegetable peeler, removing as much of the skin as possible. Seed and derib the pepper, and chop it coarsely.

In a heavy frying pan, heat the oils over medium heat. Add the red pepper, and lightly sauté for 2 minutes. Add the tomatoes, tomato paste, if you are using it, the shallot, garlic and basil, and cook, stirring frequently, until the red pepper is tender but still somewhat firm —about 5 minutes. Add the spring onion, the balsamic vinegar, salt and pepper, and simmer about 2 minutes, to bind the flavours and soften the red pepper.

Put the mixture into a food processor or blender, and purée. Chill for an hour and serve spooned on to the artichoke leaves.

EDITOR'S NOTE: *The sauce may also be used as a dip.*

Artichoke and Red Pepper Sauté with Garlic

Serves 6
Working time: about 30 minutes
Total time: about 45 minutes

Calories **75**
Protein **1g**
Cholesterol **0mg**
Total fat **7g**
Saturated fat **1g**
Sodium **100mg**

4	artichoke bottoms (page 13)	4
½	lemon	½
3 tbsp	virgin olive oil	3 tbsp
2	small garlic bulbs, cloves peeled, larger cloves halved lengthwise	2
¼ tsp	salt	¼ tsp
2	sweet red peppers	2
1½ tbsp	balsamic vinegar, or ¾ tbsp red wine vinegar mixed with ¼ tsp honey	1½ tbsp
1	shallot, finely chopped	1
½ tsp	fresh thyme, or ⅛ tsp dried thyme	½ tsp
8	large fresh basil leaves, chopped, or ½ tsp dried basil	8
	freshly ground black pepper	

Fill a large non-reactive saucepan with water and bring it to a rolling boil. Squeeze the juice of the lemon into the water and add the lemon itself. Cook the artichoke bottoms in the boiling water until they can be pierced easily with the tip of a sharp knife — 12 to 14 minutes. Plunge the artichoke bottoms into cold water to arrest their cooking, then slice each into eight wedges.

Meanwhile, in a large, heavy frying pan, heat the oil over low heat. Add the garlic and cook it, stirring occasionally, until golden — about 30 minutes. Sprinkle with ⅛ teaspoon of the salt. With a slotted spoon, transfer the garlic to a plate.

Peel the red peppers with a vegetable peeler, stripping away as much skin as possible. Seed, derib and slice the peppers into 5 mm (¼ inch) strips.

Reheat the oil over medium heat. When it is hot, add the artichoke wedges and cook them gently for 3 minutes. Stir in the red pepper, vinegar, shallot, thyme and basil. Sprinkle with the remaining salt and the pepper, and cook for 3 minutes more. Return the garlic to the frying pan and combine it with the other ingredients. Serve immediately.

Sauces for Artichokes

Yogurt and Pimiento

Serves 4
Working time: about 10 minutes
Total time: about 1 hour and 15 minutes

Calories **90**
Protein **5g**
Cholesterol **3mg**
Total fat **2g**
Saturated fat **1g**
Sodium **140mg**

4	artichokes, trimmed, cooked (pages 12 and 13) and chilled	4
15 cl	plain low-fat yogurt	¼ pint
1 tsp	Dijon mustard	1 tsp
90 g	pimientos, drained and finely chopped	3 oz
2 tsp	milk	2 tsp
1 tsp	virgin olive oil	1 tsp
1	garlic clove, finely chopped	1
1 tsp	fresh lemon juice	1 tsp
⅛ tsp	salt	⅛ tsp

In a bowl, blend together the yogurt and mustard with a whisk. Then whisk in the pimientos, milk, oil, garlic, lemon juice and salt, and refrigerate the mixture for at least an hour.

Serve the sauce with the artichokes, using the leaves to scoop it up.

Mustard

Serves 4
Working (and total) time: about 15 minutes

Calories **155**
Protein **4g**
Cholesterol **2mg**
Total fat **11g**
Saturated fat **1g**
Sodium **145mg**

4	artichokes, trimmed, cooked (pages 12 and 13) and chilled	4
1	egg white	1
1 ½ tbsp	fresh lemon juice	1 ½ tbsp
1 tbsp	Dijon mustard	1 tbsp
1 tbsp	grainy mustard	1 tbsp
1	garlic clove, finely chopped	1
2 tbsp	safflower oil	2 tbsp
1 tbsp	virgin olive oil	1 tbsp
3 tbsp	milk	3 tbsp

In a warm bowl, whisk the egg white and lemon juice to a froth. Add the mustards and garlic. Whisking vigorously, pour in the oils in a slow, thin stream. Add the milk, and whisk until the mixture thickens.

Serve the sauce with the artichokes, using the leaves to scoop it up.

Buttermilk and Tarragon

Serves 4
Working time: about 10 minutes
Total time: about 2 hours and 15 minutes

Calories **160**
Protein **4g**
Cholesterol **2mg**
Total fat **11g**
Saturated fat **1g**
Sodium **95mg**

4	artichokes, trimmed, cooked (pages 12 and 13) and chilled	4
1 tbsp	white wine vinegar	1 tbsp
½ tbsp	Dijon mustard	½ tbsp
15 cl	buttermilk	¼ pint
3 tbsp	safflower oil	3 tbsp
1	spring onion, trimmed and chopped	1
1	garlic clove, finely chopped	1
½ tsp	sugar	½ tsp
1 tbsp	chopped fresh tarragon, or 1 tsp dried tarragon	1 tbsp

In a bowl, whisk together the vinegar and mustard; then whisk in the buttermilk. Whisking vigorously, pour in the oil in a slow, thin stream. Add the spring onion, garlic, sugar and tarragon, and combine. Refrigerate the mixture for at least 2 hours.

Serve the sauce with the artichokes, using the leaves to scoop it up.

EDITOR'S NOTE: *Preparing this sauce a day in advance will intensify its flavour.*

Watercress

Serves 4
Working time: about 15 minutes
Total time: about 20 minutes

Calories **190**
Protein **3g**
Cholesterol **0mg**
Total fat **16g**
Saturated fat **2g**
Sodium **50mg**

4	artichokes, trimmed, cooked (pages 12 and 13) and chilled	4
1 tbsp	chopped shallot	1 tbsp
2 tbsp	red wine vinegar	2 tbsp
1	lime, juice only	1
1 tsp	Dijon mustard	1 tsp
	freshly ground black pepper	
1	bunch watercress, washed, stems removed	1
3 tbsp	safflower oil	3 tbsp
1 ½ tbsp	virgin olive oil	1 ½ tbsp
1	garlic clove, finely chopped	1

Bring 1 litre (1¾ pints) of water to the boil in a saucepan. Meanwhile, combine the shallot, vinegar, lime juice, mustard and pepper in a small bowl. Let the mixture stand for 10 minutes so the flavours can meld.

Blanch the watercress in the boiling water for 3 minutes. Drain and then refresh under cold running water to arrest the cooking. Squeeze the watercress to remove any excess water and coarsely chop it.

Purée the shallot mixture in a food processor or blender. With the motor still running, pour in the oils in a slow, thin stream. Add the watercress and garlic, and process for about 30 seconds. Since the vivid green of the watercress quickly fades, serve the sauce as soon as possible; use the leaves as scoops for the sauce.

Cold Asparagus with Grainy Mustard Vinaigrette

Serves 4
Working time: about 20 minutes
Total time: about 40 minutes

Calories **130**
Protein **3g**
Cholesterol **0mg**
Total fat **11g**
Saturated fat **1g**
Sodium **95mg**

20	medium asparagus spears, trimmed and peeled	20
1 tbsp	chopped shallot	1 tbsp
2 tbsp	balsamic vinegar, or 1½ tbsp red wine vinegar mixed with ½ tsp honey	2 tbsp
2 tbsp	grainy mustard	2 tbsp
3 tbsp	safflower oil	3 tbsp
4	large fresh basil leaves, sliced into thin strips, or ½ tsp dried basil	4

In a small bowl, mix together the chopped shallot and the vinegar. Let steep for about 15 minutes. Stir in the mustard. Pour in the oil in a slow, thin stream, whisking vigorously. Add the basil, and set aside.

Pour enough water into a large frying pan to fill it 2.5 cm (1 inch) deep, and bring to the boil. Line up the asparagus on the bottom, with the tips facing in one direction. Position the pan so that the thicker ends of the stalks are over the centre of the heat source, and cook the asparagus until it is tender but still crisp — about 5 minutes. Drain the asparagus and then refresh it under cold running water to arrest its cooking and to preserve its colour. Remove the asparagus from the water when cool, dry it on paper towels and refrigerate it until you are ready to serve.

At serving time, arrange the spears on individual plates or on a large serving plate. Whisk the vinaigrette again and pour it over the asparagus.

Cold Asparagus with Orange Vinaigrette

Serves 4
Working time: about 25 minutes
Total time: about 40 minutes

Calories **90**
Protein **2g**
Cholesterol **0mg**
Total fat **7g**
Saturated fat **1g**
Sodium **2mg**

20	medium asparagus spears, trimmed and peeled	20
8 cl	fresh orange juice	3 fl oz
1 tsp	fresh lime juice	1 tsp
1 tbsp	finely chopped shallot	1 tbsp
1 tsp	finely chopped garlic	1 tsp
1 tbsp	orange rind, cut into thin strips and blanched in boiling water for 30 seconds	1 tbsp
2 tbsp	virgin olive oil	2 tbsp
1 tbsp	red wine vinegar	1 tbsp

In a small bowl, mix together the orange and lime juices, the chopped shallot and garlic, and the rind. Let steep for at least 10 minutes. Whisk in the oil and vinegar, and set aside.

Pour enough water into a frying pan to fill it 2.5 cm (1 inch) deep, and bring to the boil. Line up the asparagus on the bottom, with the tips facing in one direction. Position the pan so that the thicker ends of the stalks are over the centre of the heat source, and cook the asparagus until it is tender but still crisp — about 5 minutes. Drain the asparagus and then refresh it under cold running water to arrest its cooking and to preserve its colour. Remove the asparagus from the water when cool, dry on paper towels and refrigerate until you are ready to serve.

At serving time, arrange the spears on individual plates or on a large serving plate. Whisk the vinaigrette again and pour it over the asparagus.

Stir-Fried Asparagus with Soy Sauce

Serves 4
Working time: about 25 minutes
Total time: about 30 minutes

Calories **85**
Protein **4g**
Cholesterol **0mg**
Total fat **6g**
Saturated fat **1g**
Sodium **310mg**

500 g	asparagus, trimmed and cut diagonally into 1 cm (½ inch) thick pieces	1 lb
2 tbsp	low-sodium soy sauce, or naturally fermented shoyu	2 tbsp
1½ tsp	finely chopped fresh ginger root	1½ tsp
1	garlic clove, finely chopped	1
1½ tbsp	dark sesame oil	1½ tbsp
1 tbsp	sesame seeds	1 tbsp

In a small bowl, combine the soy sauce, ginger and garlic, and set aside. In a wok or a large, heavy frying pan, heat the oil over medium-high heat. Add the soy mixture and the asparagus, and stir-fry for 3 minutes. Cover and steam the asparagus until just tender — about 2 minutes. Stir in the sesame seeds and serve immediately.

Baked Asparagus with Pine-Nuts and Gruyère

Serves 4
Working time: about 20 minutes
Total time: about 25 minutes

Calories **145**
Protein **7g**
Cholesterol **20mg**
Total fat **13g**
Saturated fat **4g**
Sodium **50mg**

500 g	medium asparagus, trimmed and peeled	1 lb
1 tsp	unsalted butter	1 tsp
60 g	grated Gruyère cheese	2 oz
3 tbsp	pine-nuts	3 tbsp
1 tbsp	virgin olive oil	1 tbsp
	freshly ground black pepper	

Preheat the oven to 180°C (350°F or Mark 4).

In a large, shallow fireproof casserole, melt the butter over medium heat. Line up the asparagus on the bottom, with the tips facing in one direction. Add 3 tablespoons of water and cover the casserole. Position it so that the thicker ends of the stalks are over the centre of the burner, and steam the asparagus for 2 minutes. Remove the casserole from the heat, and sprinkle the cheese on the stems, but not the tips. Strew the pine-nuts on the cheese, then dribble the olive oil on top. Sprinkle the asparagus with pepper.

Place the casserole in the oven, and bake, uncovered, until the cheese has melted — about 5 minutes. Serve bubbling hot.

Sweet-and-Sour Celery

Serves 4
Working time: about 10 minutes
Total time: about 15 minutes

Calories **35**
Protein **1g**
Cholesterol **0mg**
Total fat **0g**
Saturated fat **0g**
Sodium **265mg**

1	head of celery, leaves removed, stalks cut on the diagonal into 2.5 cm (1 inch) slices	1
1 tbsp	sugar	1 tbsp
¼ tsp	salt	¼ tsp
⅛ tsp	cayenne pepper	⅛ tsp
6 cl	cider vinegar	2 fl oz
1 tbsp	finely chopped sweet red pepper	1 tbsp

Pour enough water into a large frying pan to fill it about 5 mm (¼ inch) deep. Add the celery, sugar, salt and cayenne pepper. Cover the pan, leaving the lid slightly off centre to vent steam, and bring the water to the boil. Cook until the celery is tender and the water has evaporated — about 5 minutes. Remove the pan from the heat and stir in the vinegar. Transfer the sweet-and-sour celery to a serving dish and scatter the chopped red pepper over the top. Serve immediately.

Marinated Cauliflower

Serves 6
Working time: about 20 minutes
Total time: about 1 hour

Calories **85**
Protein **4g**
Cholesterol **0mg**
Total fat **5g**
Saturated fat **1g**
Sodium **105mg**

1	cauliflower head, cut into florets	1
1	onion, sliced	1
3	lemons, juice only	3
5 cm	strip of lemon peel	2 inch
8	parsley sprigs	8
3	fresh thyme sprigs, or ¼ tsp dried thyme	3
1 tsp	coriander seeds	1 tsp
½ tsp	cumin seeds	½ tsp
¼ tsp	salt	¼ tsp
10	peppercorns	10
2 tbsp	virgin olive oil	2 tbsp

Put the onion, lemon juice and peel, parsley, thyme, coriander, cumin, salt and peppercorns in a deep, non-reactive frying pan. Pour in enough water to cover the onion by 2.5 cm (1 inch). Bring the liquid to the boil over high heat, reduce the heat to medium low and simmer the liquid for 10 minutes. Raise the heat to medium high, bring the liquid once again to the boil and add the cauliflower. Cook the florets, turning them occasionally, until they are tender but not soft — about 10 minutes. Remove the pan from the

heat and let the cauliflower cool to room temperature in the liquid. Transfer it to a vegetable dish with a slotted spoon; dribble on the oil just before serving.

Braised Celery

Serves 8
Working time: about 20 minutes
Total time: about 1 hour and 20 minutes

Calories **40**
Protein **2g**
Cholesterol **0mg**
Total fat **0g**
Saturated fat **0g**
Sodium **200mg**

4	heads celery	4
1	large-sized sweet red pepper	1
1	large-sized sweet green pepper	1
275 g	carrots, peeled and thinly sliced	9 oz
1	large onion, finely chopped	1
60 cl	unsalted chicken stock	1 pint
¼ tsp	salt	¼ tsp
1 tsp	mixed dried herbs	1 tsp
	finely chopped parsley for garnish	

Trim the celery and cut each head down to about 15 cm (6 inches) long (use the trimmings for salad or soup). Remove any bruised or woody outer stalks, then cut each head in half crosswise. Wash well.

Slice the top off each pepper and remove the seeds. Wash the peppers well, and cut eight thick rings from each one. Slide one red and one green pepper ring on to each celery heart.

Scatter the sliced carrots and the chopped onion over the base of a wide shallow saucepan, arrange the celery hearts neatly on top, and pour in the chicken stock. Add the salt and sprinkle with the herbs. Bring to the boil, reduce the heat, cover and simmer until the celery is very tender — 1 to 1½ hours.

Carefully lift the celery hearts on to a serving dish, cover and keep warm. Boil the pan juices until they are reduced and slightly thickened, then pour them over the celery. Sprinkle with parsley and serve immediately.

Steamed Cauliflower with Tomato and Basil Sauce

Serves 6
Working time: about 25 minutes
Total time: about 1 hour and 10 minutes

Calories **100**
Protein **5g**
Cholesterol **5mg**
Total fat **7g**
Saturated fat **2g**
Sodium **140mg**

1	large cauliflower	1
1 tbsp	virgin olive oil	1 tbsp
1	large onion, skinned and finely chopped	1
1 kg	ripe tomatoes, skinned, seeded and roughly chopped	2 lb
2	garlic cloves, crushed	2
¼ tsp	salt	¼ tsp
2 tbsp	very finely shredded basil leaves	2 tbsp
	freshly ground black pepper	
15 g	unsalted butter	½ oz
45 g	fresh breadcrumbs	1½ oz
1 tbsp	finely cut chives	1 tbsp
2 tbsp	finely chopped parsley	2 tbsp
2 tsp	fresh thyme leaves	2 tsp
	fresh basil leaves for garnish	

Heat the oil in a large saucepan. Add the onion and cook gently until softened — about 5 minutes. Put the tomatoes, garlic, salt and basil in the pan with the onion and bring to the boil. Reduce the heat, partially cover the pan and cook gently until the tomatoes are very soft and the sauce has thickened — 45 minutes to 1 hour. Season with pepper.

Meanwhile, trim the large outer leaves from the cauliflower, and make a deep cross in the stalk. Wash the cauliflower well, then steam it gently until tender — 20 to 25 minutes.

Just before the cauliflower is cooked, melt the butter in a frying pan. Add the breadcrumbs and cook over a gentle heat, stirring continuously, until the crumbs are golden-brown. Stir in the cut chives, chopped parsley and thyme leaves.

Place the cauliflower, whole or broken into florets, in a hot serving dish. Pour the tomato sauce over the cauliflower, and sprinkle with the buttered crumbs. Garnish with basil leaves and serve immediately.

Bulb Fennel with Orange Slices

Serves 6
Working time: about 20 minutes
Total time: about 45 minutes

Calories **30**
Protein **1g**
Cholesterol **0mg**
Total fat **0g**
Saturated fat **0g**
Sodium **155mg**

3	fennel bulbs, quartered lengthwise, stems cut into 5 cm (2 inch) pieces, feathery green tops reserved	3
1	orange	1
1	onion, sliced	1
1	bay leaf	1
¼ tsp	salt	¼ tsp
	freshly ground black pepper	

With a small, sharp knife, pare the rind from the orange. In a large frying pan, combine the orange rind, fennel stems, onion, bay leaf, salt, pepper and 1 litre (1¾ pints) of water. Bring the liquid to the boil, and then simmer it over medium heat for 10 minutes.

Put the fennel quarters cut side down into the pan; cook them until tender — about 15 minutes. With a slotted spoon, transfer the quarters to a service dish and keep them warm; reserve the cooking liquid.

To make the sauce, strain the cooking liquid into a saucepan and discard the solids left in the strainer. Boil the liquid over high heat until it is reduced to ¼ litre (8 fl oz) — about 10 minutes. Using a small, sharp knife, remove the orange's bitter white pith. Then slice the orange into 5 mm (¼ inch) thick rounds and cut the rounds in half. Drain off and discard any liquid that may have collected in the serving dish holding the fennel, and pour the reduced sauce over the fennel. Arrange the orange slices on the fennel and garnish with fennel tops.

Bulb Fennel with Tomatoes and Black Olives

Serves 4
Working time: about 15 minutes
Total time: about 45 minutes

Calories **85**
Protein **2g**
Cholesterol **0mg**
Total fat **5g**
Saturated fat **1g**
Sodium **150mg**

2	fennel bulbs, green stems removed, halved lengthwise and thinly sliced	2
1 tbsp	virgin olive oil	1 tbsp
1	onion, thinly sliced	1
2	tomatoes, skinned, seeded (page 84) and coarsely chopped	2
45 g	small, whole black olives	1½ oz
10 g	fresh basil leaves, torn into small pieces, or ½ tsp dried thyme leaves	⅓ oz
	freshly ground black pepper	

Heat the oil in a large, heavy frying pan over low heat and cook the onion until translucent — 8 to 10 minutes. Add the bulb fennel and continue cooking, stirring occasionally, until the fennel is tender — about 10 minutes. Stir in the tomatoes and olives. Raise the heat to medium and cook until all the moisture has evaporated — 8 to 10 minutes more. Stir in the basil or thyme, with the pepper. Transfer the vegetables to a warmed dish and serve immediately.

Bok Choy and Ham Gratin

Serves 8
Working time: about 40 minutes
Total time: about 45 minutes

Calories **100**
Protein **7g**
Cholesterol **15mg**
Total fat **9g**
Saturated fat **6g**
Sodium **205mg**

1 kg	bok choy (Chinese chard), washed and cut into 7.5 cm (3 inch) lengths	2 lb
1½ tbsp	safflower oil	1½ tbsp
1	small onion, thinly sliced	1
1	shallot, finely chopped	1
¼ tsp	salt	¼ tsp
⅛ tsp	white pepper	⅛ tsp
2 tsp	flour	2 tsp
35 cl	milk	12 fl oz
60 g	Gruyère cheese, grated	2 oz
⅛ tsp	grated nutmeg	⅛ tsp
60 g	lean cooked ham, julienned	2 oz
1 tbsp	finely cut chives	1 tbsp

Finely chop the bok choy by hand or in a food processor. Set the bok choy aside.

In a large, heavy-bottomed frying pan, heat 1 tablespoon of the oil over medium-high heat. Add the onion and shallot and sauté them, stirring frequently, until they are just translucent — about 5 minutes. Add the bok choy, salt and pepper, and cook until the bok choy stems are slightly limp — about 5 minutes more. Remove the pan from the heat, drain off any excess liquid and set the mixture aside.

Preheat the grill. In a small bowl, whisk together the flour and the remaining oil to form a paste. Pour the milk into a small saucepan and heat it over medium heat until the surface barely trembles. Whisk the flour paste into the milk until a smooth mixture results. Whisk in the cheese and nutmeg, blend well, then stir in about three quarters of the ham.

Put the bok choy mixture in a shallow fireproof dish, pour the cheese sauce over it, and stir well to combine. Arrange the remaining ham decoratively on top. Grill the dish until the surface has browned — 2 to 3 minutes. Sprinkle with the chives; serve at once.

Broccoli and Apple Purée

Serves 6
Working (and total) time: about 30 minutes

Calories **115**
Protein **8g**
Cholesterol **5mg**
Total fat **4g**
Saturated fat **1g**
Sodium **120mg**

850 g	broccoli, stalks trimmed to 5 cm (2 inches), florets separated from stalks, stalks then peeled and cut into 1 cm (½ inch) pieces	1¾ lb
1	dessert apple, quartered and cored	1
½	lemon	½
1 tbsp	safflower oil	1 tbsp
2	shallots, coarsely chopped	2
6 cl	apple juice	2 fl oz
12.5 cl	unsalted chicken or vegetable stock	4 fl oz
1 tbsp	double cream	1 tbsp
¼ tsp	cinnamon	¼ tsp
¼ tsp	salt	¼ tsp
	freshly ground black pepper	

Pour enough water into a large saucepan to fill it about 2.5 cm (1 inch) deep. Put a vegetable steamer in the pan and bring the water to the boil. Put the broccoli florets and stalks in the steamer, and steam the broccoli, uncovered, until it is very soft — about 15 minutes. Set the broccoli aside.

Cut four thin slices from one of the apple quarters and reserve them for a garnish in a small bowl. Squeeze the lemon half over the slices to keep them from discolouring. Peel the remaining apple pieces and cut them into thin slices.

In a heavy frying pan, heat the oil over medium heat. Add the shallots and cook them, stirring occasionally, until they are translucent — 2 to 3 minutes. Stir in the peeled apple slices with the apple juice and stock, and bring the liquid to the boil.

Reduce the heat to medium low and cook the mixture, stirring occasionally, until the apples are soft — 3 to 4 minutes. Stir in the broccoli, reserving two florets for a garnish, and heat it through.

Put the broccoli-and-apple mixture into a food processor or blender. Add the cream, cinnamon, salt and pepper, and purée until smooth. (If the mixture does not contain enough liquid to yield a smooth purée, pour in 1 or 2 additional tablespoons of apple juice or stock, and process again.) Serve the purée immediately, garnished with the reserved broccoli florets and apple slices.

Broccoli with Red Pepper Sauce

Serves 4
Working (and total) time: about 15 minutes

Calories **70**
Protein **4g**
Cholesterol **0mg**
Total fat **4g**
Saturated fat **1g**
Sodium **160mg**

500 g	broccoli, stalks trimmed to 5 cm (2 inches)	1 lb
1 tbsp	virgin olive oil	1 tbsp
1	garlic clove, crushed	1
2	sweet red peppers, seeded, deribbed and coarsely chopped	2
12.5 cl	unsalted chicken or vegetable stock	4 fl oz
1½ tsp	white wine vinegar	1½ tsp
1 tbsp	chopped fresh tarragon, or 1 tsp dried tarragon	1 tbsp
1 tsp	prepared horseradish	1 tsp
¼ tsp	salt	¼ tsp
⅛ tsp	ground white pepper	⅛ tsp

Pour enough water into a saucepan to fill it 2.5 cm (1 inch) deep. Set a vegetable steamer in the pan and bring the water to the boil. Put the broccoli in the steamer, cover the pan tightly, and steam the broccoli until it is tender but still crisp — about 7 minutes.

While the broccoli is steaming, make the red pepper sauce. Heat the oil in a heavy frying pan over medium heat. Cook the garlic for 1 minute, then add the peppers and cook until they are soft — about 2 minutes. Pour in the stock and vinegar, then stir in the tarragon, horseradish, salt and pepper. As soon as the mixture reaches a simmer, remove it from the heat. Purée the mixture in a food processor or blender for about 2 minutes. Transfer the broccoli to a serving dish and strain the sauce over it. Serve immediately.

Mushrooms in Red Wine

Serves 4
Working time: about 20 minutes
Total time: about 45 minutes

Calories **170**
Protein **4g**
Cholesterol **0mg**
Total fat **7g**
Saturated fat **1g**
Sodium **155mg**

500 g	button mushrooms, stems trimmed and caps wiped clean	1 lb
¼ litre	red wine	8 fl oz
2 tbsp	virgin olive oil	2 tbsp
2 or 3	fresh thyme or rosemary sprigs, or 1 tsp dried thyme or rosemary leaves	2 or 3
¼ tsp	salt	¼ tsp
8	garlic cloves, unpeeled	8
1	bunch spring onions, white bottoms sliced, green tops finely chopped	1
2 tsp	finely chopped fresh rosemary	2 tsp
	freshly ground black pepper	

In a large saucepan, combine the wine, oil, thyme or rosemary sprigs, salt and ¼ litre (8 fl oz) of water. Bring the mixture to the boil over high heat. Reduce the heat to medium, add the garlic cloves and simmer the liquid for 10 minutes. Stir in the mushrooms and the white spring onion slices. Simmer the vegetables, partially covered, until the mushrooms feel soft when pierced with the tip of a sharp knife — about 10 minutes.

With a slotted spoon, transfer the vegetables to a serving bowl. Discard the thyme or rosemary sprigs, and boil the cooking liquid until it is reduced to about 17.5 cl (6 fl oz) — 10 to 12 minutes. Pour it over the vegetables and stir in the spring onion tops. Sprinkle the vegetables with the chopped rosemary and the pepper, and mix well. Serve the mushrooms warm or well chilled.

EDITOR'S NOTE: *Preparing this dish a day or two ahead of time will intensify its flavour and impart a deep reddish hue to the mushrooms.*

Mushroom-Walnut Pasta Roll with Yogurt Sauce

Serves 10
Working time: about 1 hour and 15 minutes
Total time: about 2 hours

Calories **215**
Protein **9g**
Cholesterol **60mg**
Total fat **11g**
Saturated fat **2g**
Sodium **160mg**

150 g	strong plain flour	5 oz
30 g	buckwheat flour	1 oz
¼ tsp	salt	¼ tsp
2	eggs, beaten	2
1 tbsp	virgin olive oil	1 tbsp
Mushroom-walnut filling		
2 tbsp	virgin olive oil	2 tbsp
1	small onion, finely chopped	1
60 g	walnuts, finely chopped	2 oz
750 g	mushrooms, wiped clean, finely chopped	1½ lb
2 tbsp	single cream	2 tbsp
1	lemon, juice only	1
25 g	parsley, finely chopped	¾ oz
¼ tsp	salt	¼ tsp
	freshly ground black pepper	
Yogurt sauce		
35 cl	plain low-fat yogurt	12 fl oz
2 tbsp	finely chopped walnuts	2 tbsp
10 g	parsley, finely chopped	⅓ oz
	freshly ground black pepper	

To prepare the dough, first sift the two flours and salt into a large mixing bowl. Make a well in the centre and pour the beaten eggs and oil into the well. With your fingers, gradually work in the flour to make a stiff paste, adding more flour if necessary. Gather the dough into a ball and knead it until it is smooth — 10 to 15 minutes. Cover the dough with a damp cloth and let it rest while you make the filling.

For the filling, heat 1 tablespoon of the oil in a large,

heavy frying pan over low heat. Add the onion, and cook it until it is soft — 10 to 12 minutes. Stir in the walnuts, and cook them for 3 or 4 minutes to toast them lightly; transfer the mixture to a large bowl.

In the same pan, heat the remaining oil, and cook the mushrooms over high heat until all the moisture has evaporated — 12 to 15 minutes. Pour in the cream, and cook for another 1 or 2 minutes; then add the lemon juice, and cook until all the liquid has evaporated — 2 to 3 minutes more. Transfer the mixture to the bowl with the onion and walnuts. Stir in the parsley, sprinkle with the salt and some pepper, and set aside to cool.

Roll the pasta dough out on a floured work surface to form a rectangle roughly 35 by 45 cm (15 by 18 inches). As you work, flip the dough over several times and dust it lightly with flour. Spread the filling in an even layer over the pasta, leaving an uncovered border 2.5 cm (1 inch) wide around the edge. Starting at a shorter edge, tightly roll up the dough and its filling, then wrap the roll in a double thickness of muslin. Tie each end with string.

Pour enough water into a fish kettle or large oval fireproof casserole to fill it 10 cm (4 inches) deep. Bring to the boil and lower the pasta roll into the water. Once the water returns to the boil, lower the heat and simmer for 45 minutes. Take the roll from the kettle, and drain it for 10 minutes before removing the string and muslin.

While the roll is draining, gently warm the yogurt — do not let it get too hot or it will curdle. Stir in the walnuts, parsley and pepper.

Slice the roll into rounds about 2 cm (¾ inch) thick and arrange them on a warmed serving platter. Serve the dish with the warmed yogurt sauce.

Ragout of Mushrooms with Madeira

Serves 4
Working time: about 30 minutes
Total time: about 1 hour and 30 minutes

Calories **135**
Protein **5g**
Cholesterol **0mg**
Total fat **4g**
Saturated fat **0g**
Sodium **155mg**

500 g	fresh mushrooms, wiped clean, stemmed and quartered	1 lb
30 g	dried shiitake mushrooms, soaked for 1 hour in warm water	1 oz
1 tbsp	safflower oil	1 tbsp
1	shallot, finely chopped	1
1	garlic clove, finely chopped	1
12.5 cl	Madeira or sherry	4 fl oz
2	tomatoes, skinned, seeded (page 84) and chopped	2
½ tsp	dried thyme leaves	½ tsp
¼ tsp	salt	¼ tsp
	freshly ground black pepper	
1 tsp	cornflour, mixed with 1 tbsp of the mushroom-soaking liquid	1 tsp
1 tbsp	chopped parsley	1 tbsp

Squeeze the excess moisture from the shiitake mushrooms and finely chop them. Heat the oil in a large, heavy frying pan over medium-high heat. Sauté the fresh mushrooms for 1 minute, then add the shallot and cook, stirring, for 30 seconds longer. Add the shiitake mushrooms and garlic, and cook for 1 minute. Pour in the Madeira or sherry, then stir in the tomatoes, thyme, salt and pepper. Cook until the mushrooms have softened — 3 to 4 minutes. Stir in the cornflour, and cook the ragout until it is slightly thickened — 1 to 2 minutes. Transfer the ragout to a serving dish and sprinkle with the chopped parsley.

EDITOR'S NOTE: *Although shiitake mushrooms are called for here, any dried wild mushroom — such as morels or ceps — may be used instead.*

Stuffed Mushrooms with Goat Cheese and Spinach

Serves 6
Working time: about 30 minutes
Total time: about 1 hour and 15 minutes

Calories **85**
Protein **3g**
Cholesterol **12mg**
Total fat **6g**
Saturated fat **3g**
Sodium **110mg**

18	large, unblemished mushrooms, wiped clean	18
6 cl	dry white wine	2 fl oz
45 g	shallots, chopped	1½ oz
1 tsp	fresh thyme, or ¼ tsp dried thyme	1 tsp
1 tbsp	fresh lime or lemon juice	1 tbsp
15 g	unsalted butter	½ oz
¼ tsp	salt	¼ tsp
1 tbsp	virgin olive oil	1 tbsp
2	garlic cloves, finely chopped	2
250 g	spinach, stems removed, leaves washed, drained, squeezed dry and coarsely chopped	8 oz
	freshly ground black pepper	
90 g	mild goat cheese	3 oz

Carefully pull out the mushroom stems and chop them finely, either by hand or in a blender or food processor. Set the mushroom caps aside.

Preheat the oven to 180°C (350°F or Mark 4). In a large frying pan, heat the wine, 8 cl (2 fl oz) of water, 2 tablespoons of the shallots and the thyme over medium heat. Bring the liquid to the boil and cook the mixture for about 3 minutes. Add the mushroom caps, bottoms facing up, and sprinkle them with the lime or lemon juice. Cover and cook until the mushrooms have shrunk by a third — 6 to 8 minutes. Remove the pan from the heat. Take the caps out of the pan one at a time, tilting them to let any juices run back into the pan. Put them on a baking sheet, bottoms down, to drain them further.

Return the pan to the stove, and reheat the contents over medium heat. Add the chopped mushroom stems, butter and half the salt; cook, stirring frequently, until all the liquid is absorbed — 6 to 8 minutes. Transfer the chopped stems to a bowl.

Wash the pan and return it to the stove. Add the oil and heat it over high heat. When the oil is hot, stir in the remaining shallots and the garlic. Immediately place the spinach on top and sprinkle with the remaining salt. Cook, stirring constantly, until all of the liquid has evaporated — about 4 minutes. Transfer the spinach mixture to the bowl containing the chopped mushroom stems, and sprinkle with pepper. Stir to combine. Break the goat cheese into small pieces directly into the bowl, then carefully fold it in.

With a teaspoon, mound the spinach-and-cheese mixture into the mushroom caps. Place them in a baking dish, and bake until they are browned on top and heated through — about 20 minutes. Serve warm.

Kohlrabies Stuffed with Dill, Yogurt and Soured Cream

Serves 4
Working time: about 30 minutes
Total time: about 1 hour and 30 minutes

Calories **195**
Protein **7g**
Cholesterol **10mg**
Total fat **10g**
Saturated fat **4g**
Sodium **230mg**

4	kohlrabies (about 1 kg/2 lb), leaves and stems removed	4
1 tbsp	safflower oil	1 tbsp
1	onion, finely chopped	1
60 g	celery, finely chopped	2 oz
2 tbsp	chopped fresh dill, or 2 tsp dried dill	2 tbsp
⅛ tsp	salt	⅛ tsp
	freshly ground black pepper	
45 g	bread cubes, from day-old French bread	1½ oz
12.5 cl	soured cream	4 fl oz
12.5 cl	plain low-fat yogurt	4 fl oz

Preheat the oven to 180°C (350°F or Mark 4). Place the kohlrabies in a lightly oiled baking dish and bake them until they feel tender when pierced with the tip of a sharp knife — 25 to 30 minutes.

Meanwhile, heat the oil in a large, heavy frying pan over medium heat. Add the chopped onion, celery and dill, and the salt and pepper, and cook until the vegetables are soft — 7 to 10 minutes. Remove the pan from the heat and set aside.

Slice the woody tops off the kohlrabies and discard them. Carefully hollow out each kohlrabi, leaving the walls about 5 mm (¼ inch) thick. Chop the scooped-out flesh and mix it with the vegetables in the pan. Stir in the bread cubes, soured cream and yogurt. Fill the kohlrabi shells with the mixture, then return them to the baking dish and bake them until they are heated through — 10 to 15 minutes.

Garnish each of the stuffed kohlrabies with a sprig of dill before serving.

Swiss Chard and Three-Onion Stew

Serves 8
Working (and total) time: about 1 hour

Calories **105**
Protein **3g**
Cholesterol **10mg**
Total fat **5g**
Saturated fat **2g**
Sodium **145mg**

1 kg	Swiss chard, washed, the stems cut into 1 cm (½ inch) pieces, the leaves coarsely shredded	2 lb
1	large carrot, peeled and cut into 5 mm (¼ inch) cubes	1
35 cl	unsalted chicken or vegetable stock	12 fl oz
350 g	potatoes, peeled and cut into 5 mm (¼ inch) cubes	12 oz
25 g	unsalted butter	¾ oz
1 tbsp	safflower oil	1 tbsp
1	red onion, coarsely chopped	1
2	small leeks, trimmed, cleaned (page 110) and cut crosswise into 5 mm (¼ inch) slices	2
4	spring onions, trimmed and cut into 5 mm (¼ inch) slices	4
¼ tsp	salt	¼ tsp
½	lemon, juice only	½
	freshly ground black pepper	
1 tbsp	finely chopped parsley (optional)	1 tbsp

Pour enough water into a large saucepan to fill it about 1 cm (½ inch) deep. Drop in the carrot, cover the pan and bring the water to the boil; cook the carrot for 5 minutes. Add the chard stems and cook them, covered, until they are tender — 3 to 5 minutes. Then add the shredded chard leaves and cook them, covered, for 3 minutes. Remove the pan from the heat and let the vegetables sit uncovered to cool.

In a small saucepan, combine the stock and the potato cubes. Cover the pan, bring the liquid to the boil and cook until the potatoes are very tender — about 10 minutes. Drain the potatoes, reserving the stock, and then purée them in a food mill or through a fine-meshed sieve. Stir the stock into the puréed potatoes and set aside.

In a large pan, heat the butter and oil over medium heat. Add the onion, leeks and spring onions, and toss to coat them evenly. Cover the pan and cook the onions, stirring occasionally, until they are soft — about 5 minutes. Stir in the chard mixture and the salt, re-cover the pan, and cook, stirring occasionally, for 10 minutes.

Spoon the potato purée into the pan, mix well, and cook until the stew is heated through. Stir in the lemon juice and pepper. Garnish with the parsley, if using, and serve at once.

Swiss Chard with Ham

Serves 6
Working time: about 20 minutes
Total time: about 30 minutes

Calories **45**
Protein **4g**
Cholesterol **5mg**
Total fat **2g**
Saturated fat **1g**
Sodium **200mg**

1 kg	Swiss chard, washed, the stems cut into 1 cm (½ inch) pieces, the leaves coarsely shredded	2 lb
1	onion, chopped	1
½ tsp	dried oregano	½ tsp
	freshly ground black pepper	
½ litre	unsalted chicken or vegetable stock	16 fl oz
60 g	smoked ham, shredded	2 oz
1 tbsp	white wine vinegar	1 tbsp

In a large saucepan with a tight-fitting lid, combine the chard stems, onion, oregano, pepper and stock. Bring the liquid to the boil, then reduce the heat to low, and simmer until the stems are tender — about 5 minutes. Remove the stems and onion from the stock with a slotted spoon and keep them warm.

Drop the chard leaves into the stock, cover the pan and return the stock to the boil. Cook the leaves until they are tender — about 3 minutes. Without turning off the heat, use a slotted spoon to transfer the leaves to a heated platter. Scatter the stems and onion over the leaves and keep the dish warm.

Add the ham and vinegar to the boiling stock and cook until the liquid is reduced by half — about 5 minutes. Pour the stock mixture over the vegetables and serve at once.

Bean Sprout Sauté

Serves 4
Working (and total) time: about 20 minutes

Calories **100**
Protein **2g**
Cholesterol **0mg**
Total fat **7g**
Saturated fat **1g**
Sodium **285mg**

125 g	fresh bean sprouts	4 oz
2 tbsp	safflower oil	2 tbsp
½ tsp	salt	½ tsp
¼ tsp	white pepper	¼ tsp
150 g	large yellow courgettes, halved lengthwise, seeded and shredded into long strips with a grater	5 oz
125 g	medium carrot, peeled and shredded into long strips with a grater	4 oz
2	spring onions, trimmed, cut into 5 cm (2 inch) pieces, sliced lengthwise	2
1 tbsp	cream sherry	1 tbsp

In a large, heavy frying pan, heat the oil over high heat. Sauté the bean sprouts for 1 minute. Sprinkle them with half the salt and pepper. Add the courgettes, carrot and spring onions, and sauté until the carrots are tender — about 2 minutes. Stir in the remaining salt and pepper. Remove the pan from the heat. Add the sherry and toss to incorporate. Serve the dish immediately.

2 *Wrapped in leaves, a red cabbage tart with onion and prunes (recipe, page 42) is surrounded by fanciful interpretations of the most basic of leafy vegetables.*

The Bounty of the Greens

The leafy vegetables are among the most nourishing of all fresh produce. Always in abundant supply in the markets, they contain high levels of vitamins A and C, and can be a good source of thiamine, riboflavin and such essential minerals as iron and calcium as well. (A portion of cooked kale can offer almost the entire Recommended Daily Amount of both vitamins A and C.) At the same time, leafy vegetables contribute fibre to the diet, and among them particularly so kale and spinach. It is no wonder that nutritionists have recommended the eating of dark-green leafy vegetables at least three times a week.

The variety of leafy vegetables reaching the markets has greatly increased in recent years to allow an enlargement of any enterprising cook's repertoire. And they can be the basis for experimentation too. For example, Savoy cabbage, one of the most widely grown and inexpensive vegetables available, is in this section hollowed out and stuffed with chicken and apple. And the shorter cooking time recommended for leafy vegetables generally conserves more of the nutrients than does the older method of boiling the greens for an extended period.

The section also takes some greens normally not considered vegetables and transforms them into main courses. Cos lettuce leaves become the wrappers for packages of shredded cucumber, carrot and yellow squash, flavoured lightly with dark sesame oil and then gently steamed. Batavian endive acquires another identity when baked with rosemary-seasoned layers of potatoes and onions. Watercress emerges newborn in a colourful timbale made with sweetcorn and diced pimiento. And that familiar garnish parsley, like a typecast actor throwing off the shackles of a tired characterization, plays a different role as the base for a wonderfully satisfying dish made with burghul cooked in orange juice, then tossed with orange segments and grated radishes. These dishes, plus the 21 others that follow for leafy vegetables, were devised to show that healthy food can be as delicious as it is nutritious.

Brussels Sprouts with Caramelized Onion

Serves 4
Working time: about 15 minutes
Total time: about 1 hour and 30 minutes

Calories **150**
Protein **7g**
Cholesterol **0mg**
Total fat **4g**
Saturated fat **1g**
Sodium **90mg**

500 g	Brussels sprouts, cut in half	1 lb
1	large onion, thinly sliced	1
1 tbsp	virgin olive oil	1 tbsp
⅛ tsp	salt	⅛ tsp
	freshly ground black pepper	
¼ litre	dry white wine	8 fl oz

Put the onion, oil, salt, pepper, and 12 cl (4 fl oz) of water in a saucepan. Bring the water to the boil over high heat and partially cover the pan so that a little steam can escape. Reduce the heat to medium and cook the onion, stirring occasionally, until it is caramelized — about 1 hour.

Uncover the pan and add the wine to the onion. Raise the heat to high and boil rapidly until almost all the wine has evaporated — 5 to 10 minutes.

About 15 minutes before the onion is done, steam the Brussels sprouts. Pour enough water into a saucepan to fill it 2.5 cm (1 inch) deep. Set a vegetable steamer in the pan and bring the water to the boil. Put the Brussels sprouts in the steamer, cover the pan tightly, and steam the sprouts until tender — about 5 minutes. Toss the onion with the Brussels sprouts and serve.

Brussels Sprouts and Noodles with Dill

Serves 6
Working time: about 10 minutes
Total time: about 20 minutes

Calories **140**
Protein **6g**
Cholesterol **10mg**
Total fat **4g**
Saturated fat **2g**
Sodium **125mg**

300 g	Brussels sprouts, quartered	10 oz
6 cl	plain low-fat yogurt	2 fl oz
6 cl	soured cream	2 fl oz
1 tbsp	chopped fresh dill, or 1 tsp dried dill	1 tbsp
¼ tsp	salt	¼ tsp
	freshly ground black pepper	
125 g	egg noodles	4 oz
15 g	butter	½ oz

Mix together the yogurt, soured cream, dill, salt and pepper in a small bowl and set aside.

Bring 3 litres (5½ pints) of water to the boil in a large saucepan. Boil the noodles in the water until they are cooked — about 5 minutes.

In the meantime, pour enough water into another saucepan to fill it 2.5 cm (1 inch) deep. Set a vegetable steamer in the pan and bring the water to the boil. Put the sprouts in the steamer, cover the saucepan tightly, and steam the sprouts until tender — about 5 minutes.

When the noodles are done, drain them and toss them with the butter. Stir in the sprouts and the yogurt and soured cream mixture. Transfer the sprouts and noodles to a warmed dish, and serve immediately.

Creamy Mustard Greens

Serves 6
Working time: about 35 minutes
Total time: about 55 minutes

Calories **125**
Protein **5g**
Cholesterol **15mg**
Total fat **8g**
Saturated fat **4g**
Sodium **150mg**

1 kg	mustard greens, washed, stemmed and coarsely chopped	2 lb
30 g	unsalted butter	1 oz
3 tbsp	chopped shallots	3 tbsp
1	garlic clove, finely chopped	1
¼ tsp	salt	¼ tsp
1 tbsp	safflower oil	1 tbsp
2 tbsp	flour	2 tbsp
40 cl	semi-skimmed milk	14 fl oz
¼ tsp	grated nutmeg	¼ tsp
	freshly ground black pepper	

In a large, heavy saucepan, melt the butter over medium heat. Add the shallots and garlic, and cook for 1 minute. Stir in the greens and the salt; cook, stirring frequently, until almost all the liquid has evaporated — about 15 minutes. Cover and set aside.

In a small saucepan, heat the oil over medium heat. Add the flour and whisk until the mixture begins to bubble, then cook, stirring for 3 minutes more. Blend in the milk and cook, whisking constantly to prevent lumps, for about 3 minutes. Reduce the heat to low. Add the nutmeg and pepper, and continue to cook, whisking frequently, for 10 minutes more. Pour the sauce into the pan with the greens and toss to coat thoroughly. Serve immediately.

EDITOR'S NOTE: *Mustard greens, also known as green-in-snow or Chinese mustard, are not yet widely available though increasingly grown by home gardeners. Spinach or Swiss chard leaves could be used instead.*

Beet Greens with Vinegar and Caraway

Serves 4
Working time: about 30 minutes
Total time: about 1 hour and 30 minutes

Calories **55**
Protein **2g**
Cholesterol **0mg**
Total fat **0g**
Saturated fat **0g**
Sodium **165mg**

2 kg	medium beetroots with tops	4 lb
6 cl	cider vinegar	2 fl oz
1	garlic clove, finely chopped	1
¼ tsp	caraway seeds	¼ tsp
⅛ tsp	salt	⅛ tsp

Preheat the oven to 200°C (400°F or Mark 6). Cut the greens off all the beetroots, leaving 5 cm (2 inches) of stem, and reserve half the beetroots for another use. Wash the others, and all the greens. Remove the stems from the greens and discard; cut the leaves crosswise into 2.5 cm (1 inch) wide strips and set them aside.

Wrap the beetroots in aluminium foil in one package and bake them until tender — about 1 hour. Unwrap the beetroots and let them cool. Peel and then slice the beetroots into 5 mm (¼ inch) rounds, and set them aside.

Put the vinegar, garlic, caraway seeds and salt into a small saucepan and bring the liquid to the boil. Reduce the liquid by half and set it aside.

Pour 2 tablespoons of water into a large pan and add the beet greens. Cover the pan and bring the water to the boil, then uncover the pan and cook the greens until they are wilted — about 1 minute. Pour out any remaining liquid. Add the vinegar mixture and the baked beetroots to the pan, and toss the beetroots until they are heated through. Serve immediately.

EDITOR'S NOTE: *Beet greens are sometimes sold separately.*

Stir-Fried Chinese Cabbage and Plantain

ALTHOUGH TECHNICALLY A FRUIT, PLANTAINS ARE USED
THROUGHOUT LATIN AMERICA AND SOUTH-EAST ASIA AS A
STARCHY VEGETABLE. PLANTAINS MUST BE COOKED BEFORE
THEY CAN BE EATEN.

Serves 6
Working (and total) time: about 10 minutes

Calories **75**
Protein **3g**
Cholesterol **0mg**
Total fat **2g**
Saturated fat **0g**
Sodium **5mg**

1 kg	Chinese cabbage, shredded	2 lb
1 tbsp	safflower oil	1 tbsp
4	spring onions, sliced diagonally into 1 cm (½ inch) pieces	4
1	ripe plantain, sliced into thin rounds	1
½ tsp	crushed red pepper flakes	½ tsp
3 tbsp	rice vinegar or cider vinegar	3 tbsp

In a wok or a large, heavy-bottomed frying pan, heat the oil over high heat. Add the spring onion and plantain pieces and stir-fry for 1 minute. Add the cabbage and red pepper flakes; cook, stirring constantly, until the cabbage wilts — 1 to 2 minutes more. Pour in the vinegar and cook for 1 minute. Transfer the cabbage and plantain to a large dish and serve immediately.

Marinated Red and Green Cabbage

Serves 8
Working time: about 30 minutes
Total time: about 4 hours and 30 minutes

Calories **120**
Protein **2g**
Cholesterol **0mg**
Total fat **4g**
Saturated fat **0g**
Sodium **155mg**

500 g	red cabbage, shredded	1 lb
500 g	green cabbage, shredded	1 lb
2	large carrots, grated	2
1	large red onion, very thinly sliced	1
2 tbsp	finely chopped fresh ginger root	2 tbsp
¼ litre	cider vinegar	8 fl oz
90 g	sultanas	3 oz
3 tbsp	honey	3 tbsp
2 tbsp	safflower oil	2 tbsp
½ tsp	salt	½ tsp
3	spring onions, trimmed and sliced	3
	freshly ground black pepper	

Pour enough water into a large saucepan to fill it about 2.5 cm (1 inch) deep. Place a vegetable steamer in the pan and bring the water to the boil. Put the cabbage and carrots in the steamer, cover the pot tightly, and steam the vegetables, stirring them once, for 5 minutes. Drain the vegetables well and transfer them to a mixing bowl. Add the onion, ginger and vinegar, and toss. Set the vegetables aside to marinate for at least 4 hours.

Squeeze the marinated vegetables a handful at a time over a saucepan to catch the juices; as you work, transfer the drained vegetables to a bowl. Boil the liquid over high heat until it has reduced to 12.5 cl (4 fl oz) — about 5 minutes. Add the sultanas and remove the pan from the heat. When the liquid has cooled, whisk in the honey, oil and salt. Pour the sauce over the drained vegetables, and stir in the spring onions and pepper. Serve chilled or at room temperature.

Cabbage Rolls with Barley and Tomatoes

Serves 8 as a side dish, 4 as a main course
Working time: about 1 hour
Total time: about 2 hours

Calories **120**
Protein **4g**
Cholesterol **5mg**
Total fat **5g**
Saturated fat **1g**
Sodium **120mg**

8	large green cabbage leaves	8
3	large tomatoes, cored	3
100 g	pearl barley, rinsed under cold running water and drained	3½ oz
1½ tsp	dried oregano, or 3 tsp chopped fresh oregano	1½ tsp
2	garlic cloves, quartered	2
6 cl	red wine vinegar or cider vinegar	2 fl oz
2 tbsp	safflower oil	2 tbsp
1 tbsp	sugar	1 tbsp
150 g	courgettes, cut into 1 cm (½ inch) cubes	5 oz
¼ tsp	salt	¼ tsp
	freshly ground black pepper	
3	spring onions, trimmed, cut into 1 cm (½ inch) lengths	3
30 g	Parmesan cheese, freshly grated	1 oz

In a large pan, bring 1 litre (1¾ pints) of water to the boil. Meanwhile, cut a shallow cross on the bottom of each tomato. Immerse the tomatoes in the boiling water. As soon as the tomato skins begin to peel away from the crosses — about 30 seconds — remove the tomatoes with a slotted spoon and set them aside.

Immediately add the barley and half the oregano to the boiling water; reduce the heat to medium high and cook, covered, until all the water is absorbed — about 45 minutes. Transfer the barley to a bowl.

While the barley is cooking, skin and seed the tomatoes as shown on page 84, then coarsely chop them. Place the chopped tomatoes, the garlic, vinegar, 1 tablespoon of the oil and the sugar in a blender or food processor, and purée until smooth.

In another large pan, bring 2 litres (3½ pints) of water to the boil. Add the cabbage leaves and cook them, uncovered, until they are limp — 8 to 10 minutes. Drain the leaves. When they are cool enough to handle, ▶

cut the thick core from the base of each cabbage leaf, then set the leaves aside.

In a large, heavy frying pan, heat the remaining oil over medium-high heat. Add the courgettes, the remaining oregano, the salt and pepper. Sauté the courgettes for 3 minutes, stirring frequently, then add the spring onions and cook for 30 seconds more. Pour all but 12.5 cl (4 fl oz) of the puréed tomatoes into the pan; cook the mixture, stirring occasionally, until it has thickened — about 10 minutes. Add the contents of the pan to the bowl with the barley. Sprinkle in the grated Parmesan cheese and stir well to combine the mixture.

Place about one eighth of the barley-and-tomato mixture at the stem end of a cabbage leaf. Roll up the leaf from stem to tip, turning in the sides of the leaf after the first roll *(leaf-rolling technique, page 51)*. Repeat the process with the other leaves, distributing the barley mixture evenly among them.

Pour the reserved tomato purée into a large frying pan with a lid. Place the cabbage rolls, seam side down, in the pan. Cover the pan and cook the rolls over low heat for 15 minutes. Serve immediately.

Red Cabbage Tart

Serves 6
Working time: about 20 minutes
Total time: about 1 hour and 45 minutes

Calories **105**
Protein **2g**
Cholesterol **5mg**
Total fat **6g**
Saturated fat **1g**
Sodium **110mg**

1 kg	red cabbage	2 lb
6 tbsp	red wine vinegar	6 tbsp
2 tbsp	safflower oil	2 tbsp
1	large red onion, finely chopped	1
¼ tsp	salt	¼ tsp
6	prunes, stoned and coarsely chopped	6
⅛ tsp	ground cloves	⅛ tsp
1 tsp	unsalted butter	1 tsp

Pour 6 litres (10 pints) of water and 4 tablespoons of the vinegar into a large, non-reactive saucepan; bring the liquid to the boil. Remove 10 outer leaves from the cabbage and put them in the boiling water. When the water returns to the boil, reduce the heat to medium and simmer the leaves until they are tender — 10 to 15 minutes. Drain the leaves and refresh them under cold running water until they are cool.

While the leaves are simmering, quarter, core and finely shred the remaining cabbage. In a large, heavy, fireproof casserole, heat the oil over medium-low heat. Cook the onion until it is soft — about 10 minutes. Stir in the shredded cabbage and the salt. Simmer the mixture, covered, for about 15 minutes. Stir in the prunes and cloves. Continue cooking the mixture, covered, until the cabbage and the prunes are very soft — about 15 minutes more. Stir in the remaining vinegar.

Preheat the oven to 180°C (350°F or Mark 4). Rub the inside of a 20 to 23 cm (8 to 9 inch) glass or earthenware pie dish with half of the butter. Arrange all but two or three of the cabbage leaves in the bottom of the dish, with the stem ends pointing outwards; allow the stem ends to hang over the edge of the dish somewhat. Mound the cabbage-and-prune mixture in the centre

and fold the stem ends securely over the top. Cover the top with the reserved leaves. Dot the top with the remaining butter.

Cover the dish with foil and bake the tart until it is tender and all the moisture has been absorbed — 45 minutes to 1 hour. Invert the tart on to a warmed plate and slice it into serving wedges.

Steamed Chinese Cabbage with Green Pepper

Serves 6
Working time: about 10 minutes
Total time: about 25 minutes

Calories **25**
Protein **2g**
Cholesterol **0mg**
Total fat **0g**
Saturated fat **0g**
Sodium **90mg**

1 kg	Chinese cabbage, thinly sliced	2 lb
1 tsp	Sichuan peppercorns, or ½ tsp freshly ground black pepper	1 tsp
6 cl	cider vinegar	2 fl oz
1 tbsp	dark brown sugar	1 tbsp
½ tsp	crushed red pepper flakes	½ tsp
¼ tsp	salt	¼ tsp
1	sweet green pepper, seeded, deribbed and thinly sliced	1

In a small, heavy frying pan, toast the Sichuan peppercorns over medium heat for 3 to 4 minutes, shaking the pan frequently. Transfer the peppercorns to a work surface and crush them. Combine the vinegar, brown sugar, Sichuan or black pepper, red pepper flakes, salt and 6 cl (2 fl oz) of water in a small saucepan. Bring the liquid to the boil over high heat, and cook it rapidly to reduce it by half — 4 to 5 minutes. Remove the sauce from the heat and set it aside.

Pour enough water into a large pan to fill it about 2.5 cl (1 inch) deep. Put a vegetable steamer in the pan and bring the water to the boil. Put the sliced cabbage and green pepper in the steamer, cover the pan tightly, and steam the vegetables until the cabbage is just barely wilted — about 3 minutes.

Transfer the vegetables to a serving bowl and pour the sauce through a strainer on to them. Toss the vegetables well and let them stand for 5 minutes before serving.

Savoy Cabbage Stuffed with Chicken and Apple

Serves 4 as a main course
Working time: about 45 minutes
Total time: about 1 hour and 40 minutes

Calories **240**
Protein **17g**
Cholesterol **50mg**
Total fat **11g**
Saturated fat **4g**
Sodium **190mg**

One 2 kg	firm Savoy cabbage, outer leaves discarded	One 4 lb
1 tbsp	safflower oil	1 tbsp
300 g	onion, chopped	10 oz
1 tbsp	caraway seeds	1 tbsp
¼ tsp	salt	¼ tsp
	freshly ground black pepper	
6 tbsp	balsamic vinegar, or 4 tbsp red wine vinegar mixed with 2 tbsp water	6 tbsp
1 tsp	honey	1 tsp
25 g	unsalted butter	¾ oz
1	large dessert apple, cored and cut into 1 cm (½ inch) pieces	1
1 tbsp	fresh lemon juice	1 tbsp
250 g	chicken breast meat, cut into 1 cm (½ inch) cubes	8 oz
45 g	parsley sprigs	1½ oz

Hollow out the cabbage as demonstrated below. Chop enough of the scooped-out leaves to yield about 250 g (8 oz), and set them aside.

In a large, heavy frying pan, heat the oil over medium heat. Add the onion and caraway seeds, and cook them for 2 minutes. Stir in the chopped cabbage and the salt and pepper; cook, stirring frequently, for 5 minutes. Pour in 4 tablespoons of the vinegar and the honey, and cook the mixture for 5 minutes more. Transfer the mixture to a large bowl.

Melt the butter in the pan over medium-high heat. When the butter bubbles, add the apple pieces and sauté them, stirring frequently, for 3 minutes. Add the lemon juice and chicken cubes, and cook, stirring constantly, for 2 minutes. Add the remaining vinegar, the parsley and some additional pepper, and sauté for 1 minute more to combine the flavours. Transfer the mixture to the bowl with the cabbage and mix well.

Fill the cabbage shell with the stuffing and replace the reserved cabbage lid. Set a rack in a large pan with a tight-fitting lid. Pour enough water into the pan to fill it about 2.5 cm (1 inch) deep. Place the stuffed cabbage, stem end down, on the rack, and bring the water to the boil. Cover the pan, reduce the heat to medium low, and steam the cabbage for 40 minutes. Remove the cabbage from the pan and cut it into serving wedges.

Hollowing a Whole Cabbage for Stuffing

1 *SCOOPING OUT THE CENTRE. Trim the protruding stem of the cabbage just enough to allow the cabbage to be stood on end. Cut a lid about 10 cm (4 inches) in diameter and 1 cm (½ inch) thick off the top of the cabbage and set it aside. With a sturdy tablespoon, dig into the exposed centre and scoop out the loosened leaves until the cabbage walls are about 2.5 cm (1 inch) thick.*

2 *REMOVING THE INNER LEAVES. Carefully remove whole leaves from the inner walls by snapping them off at the base with your fingers; continue until the walls of the cabbage are only about 1 cm (½ inch) thick. Reserve the loosened leaves for the stuffing.*

Spring Greens with Smoked Turkey

Serves 4
Working time: about 20 minutes
Total time: about 30 minutes

Calories **110**
Protein **7g**
Cholesterol **10mg**
Total fat **5g**
Saturated fat **1g**
Sodium **230mg**

600 g	spring greens, washed, stems and centre ribs removed, leaves coarsely chopped	1¼ lb
1 tbsp	safflower oil	1 tbsp
1	onion, thinly sliced	1
1	apple, peeled, cored and grated	1
⅛ tsp	salt	⅛ tsp
	freshly ground black pepper	
15 cl	unsalted chicken or vegetable stock	5 fl oz
90 g	smoked turkey breast	3 oz

Heat the oil in a large, heavy frying pan over medium heat. Add the onion and cook until it turns translucent — about 5 minutes. Stir in the spring greens, apple, salt and pepper, and cook for 1 minute. Pour in the stock and simmer for 5 to 10 minutes, or until tender. Stir in the turkey and cook 5 minutes more. Serve immediately.

EDITOR'S NOTE: *Swiss chard leaves can be used instead of spring greens, both here and in the following recipe.*

Spring Greens with Sultanas and Pine-Nuts

Serves 4
Working time: about 25 minutes
Total time: about 40 minutes

Calories **125**
Protein **6g**
Cholesterol **0mg**
Total fat **6g**
Saturated fat **1g**
Sodium **170mg**

500 g	spring greens, washed, stems and centre ribs removed, leaves cut into 1 cm (½ inch) wide strips	1 lb
1	garlic clove, finely chopped	1
1 tbsp	pine-nuts	1 tbsp
45 g	sultanas	1½ oz
¼ tsp	anchovy paste or salt	¼ tsp
1 tbsp	virgin olive oil	1 tbsp
	freshly ground black pepper	
2 tbsp	chopped parsley	2 tbsp
1	lemon, cut in wedges	1

Put the greens, garlic and ¼ litre (8 fl oz) of water in a large saucepan. Cover the pan tightly, bring the water to the boil, and cook the greens over medium-high heat for 5 minutes. In a small, heavy frying pan, toast the pine-nuts over medium-high heat until they are golden — 1 to 2 minutes. Set aside.

Stir the sultanas, the anchovy paste or salt, and a little water if necessary, into the spring greens. Cover the pan again, reduce the heat to medium, and cook the greens for 5 minutes more.

Uncover the pan and continue cooking until any excess liquid evaporates — about 5 minutes. Add the pine-nuts, oil, pepper and parsley, and toss the greens. Transfer to a dish and garnish with the lemon wedges.

Batavian Endive and Potato Gratin with Rosemary

Serves 10
Working time: about 45 minutes
Total time: about 1 hour and 45 minutes

Calories **125**
Protein **3g**
Cholesterol **5mg**
Total fat **4g**
Saturated fat **1g**
Sodium **125mg**

750 g	Batavian endive, washed, trimmed and coarsely chopped	1 ½ lb
1 kg	potatoes	2 lb
2 tbsp	virgin olive oil	2 tbsp
500 g	onions, thinly sliced	1 lb
½ tsp	salt	½ tsp
	freshly ground black pepper	
3	garlic cloves, finely chopped	3
2 tbsp	chopped fresh rosemary, or 1 ½ tsp dried rosemary, crumbled	2 tbsp
6 cl	half milk, half cream	2 fl oz

Preheat the oven to 220°C (425°F or Mark 7). Peel the potatoes, halve them lengthwise and slice them thinly. To keep the slices from discolouring, put them in a bowl and pour in enough water to cover. Set aside.

In a large, deep, heavy frying pan, heat 1 tablespoon of the olive oil over medium-low heat. Add the sliced onions and ¼ teaspoon of the salt; cook, stirring frequently, until the onions are translucent — about 10 minutes. Then stir the chopped Batavian endive and some pepper into the pan. Cook, stirring constantly, until the endive has wilted —about 2 minutes more. Remove the pan from the heat.

Drain the potatoes well and return them to the bowl. Add the remaining oil, the garlic, rosemary and remaining salt, and toss the mixture well.

Spread half of the potatoes over the bottom of a 23 by 33 cm (9 by 13 inch) baking tin. Distribute the endive and onions evenly on top and cover them with the remaining potato mixture. Cover the dish with aluminium foil and bake it for 30 minutes.

Remove the dish from the oven, lift off the foil and pour the milk and cream mixture evenly over the contents. Return the uncovered dish to the oven and bake it until the top layer of potatoes is lightly browned and the potatoes on the bottom are tender when pierced with a fork — about 30 minutes more. Remove from the oven and serve immediately.

Chicory with Parsley Sauce

Serves 6
Working time: about 20 minutes
Total time: about 1 hour and 15 minutes

Calories **65**
Protein **3g**
Cholesterol **10mg**
Total fat **3g**
Saturated fat **2g**
Sodium **95mg**

12	small heads chicory	12
½ litre	unsalted chicken stock	16 fl oz
1	bouquet garni, made with 6 parsley stems, 2 thyme sprigs and 1 bay leaf	1
6 cl	fresh lemon juice	2 fl oz
45 g	parsley leaves	1½ oz
8 cl	single cream	3 fl oz
⅛ tsp	salt	⅛ tsp
	freshly ground white pepper	

In a large non-reactive pan, bring the stock to the boil. Add the bouquet garni, cover the pan, and simmer the stock for 10 minutes. Add the lemon juice and chicory, and re-cover. Simmer until the chicory feels tender when pierced at the base with a sharp knife tip — 20 to 25 minutes. With a slotted spoon, transfer the chicory to a serving dish and keep it warm. Discard the bouquet garni, and boil the liquid until it is reduced to about 15 cl (¼ pint) — 15 to 20 minutes.

While the liquid is reducing, blanch the parsley leaves for 1 minute in boiling water and drain them. Purée the leaves in a food processor or a blender. With the motor still running, slowly pour the reduced cooking liquid into the puréed parsley and blend well. Strain the sauce into a small saucepan set over low heat, and stir in the cream, salt and pepper. Drain off any liquid that may have collected in the serving dish, and pour the parsley sauce over the chicory. Serve immediately.

Braised Chicory with Apple

Serves 4
Working time: about 10 minutes
Total time: about 25 minutes

Calories **80**
Protein **2g**
Cholesterol **0mg**
Total fat **4g**
Saturated fat **0g**
Sodium **85mg**

500 g	chicory, cut into 2.5 cm (1 inch) slices	1 lb
1	red apple, cut into eighths then into 1 cm (½ inch) slices	1
1	lemon, juice only	1
1 tbsp	safflower oil	1 tbsp
⅛ tsp	salt	⅛ tsp
	freshly ground black pepper	
2 tbsp	cider vinegar	2 tbsp

Place the chicory, apple, lemon juice, oil, salt, pepper and 17.5 cl (6 fl oz) of water in a heavy frying pan. Cover and bring to the boil over high heat. Steam the chicory until it is tender — about 10 minutes. Uncover the pan and cook 1 or 2 minutes to evaporate the water. Reduce the heat to medium and cook until the chicory is browned — about 5 minutes. Pour the vinegar over the chicory, stir well and remove the pan from the heat. Transfer the chicory to a vegetable dish and serve.

Watercress Timbale with Sweetcorn and Pimiento

A TIMBALE IS A CREAMY MIXTURE OF VEGETABLES OR MEAT,
BAKED IN A MOULD.

Serves 4
Working time: about 25 minutes
Total time: about 45 minutes

Calories **65**
Protein **4g**
Cholesterol **70mg**
Total fat **2g**
Saturated fat **1g**
Sodium **170mg**

2	bunches watercress, washed, thick ends of stems cut off	2
175 g	fresh sweetcorn kernels (about 1 large ear), or 175 g (6 oz) frozen sweetcorn kernels, thawed	6 oz
1	egg	1
8 cl	skimmed milk	3 fl oz
1/8 tsp	grated nutmeg	1/8 tsp
1/4 tsp	salt	1/4 tsp
1/4 tsp	white pepper	1/4 tsp
30 g	finely diced pimiento	1 oz

Place the watercress, with water still clinging to it, in a saucepan. Cover the pan and steam the watercress over medium heat until it is slightly wilted — about 1 minute.

Plunge the watercress into cold water to arrest the cooking. When the watercress is cool, drain it and use your hands to squeeze out any excess liquid. Set the watercress aside.

Pour enough water into a saucepan to fill it about 2.5 cm (1 inch) deep. Set a vegetable steamer in the pan and bring the water to the boil. Put the sweetcorn in the steamer, cover the pan, and steam the sweetcorn until it is tender — about 4 minutes. Set aside.

Preheat the oven to 170°C (325°F or Mark 3). Place the watercress, egg, milk, nutmeg, salt and pepper in a food processor or blender, and process for about 5 minutes, stopping a few times to scrape down the sides. Transfer the purée to a bowl and mix in the sweetcorn.

Lightly butter the inside of four 175 g (6 oz) ramekins. Distribute the pimiento pieces evenly among the ramekins, then fill the ramekins with the purée mixture. Put the ramekins in a shallow ovenproof baking dish and pour enough boiling water into the dish to come half way up the sides of the ramekins. Bake until the timbales are nearly firm in the centre — about 20 minutes.

Allow the timbales to cool slightly, then rap the bottom of each ramekin against a hard surface and invert the timbales on to individual serving plates. Serve the watercress timbales warm.

Kale Calzones

A CALZONE IS A SEMICIRCULAR POCKET OF PIZZA DOUGH,
STUFFED WITH MEAT OR VEGETABLES, SEALED AND BAKED.

Serves 4 as a main course
Working time: about 1 hour
Total time: about 2 hours and 30 minutes

Calories **515**
Protein **17g**
Cholesterol **15mg**
Total fat **17g**
Saturated fat **4g**
Sodium **345mg**

500 g	kale, washed and stemmed	1 lb
2	tomatoes, skinned, seeded (page 84) and chopped	2
2	red onions, chopped	2
2	small carrots, peeled, quartered lengthwise and cut into 1 cm (½ inch) pieces	2
8 cl	red wine vinegar or cider vinegar	3 fl oz
2	garlic cloves, chopped	2
1 tbsp	chopped fresh sage, or ¾ tsp dried sage	1 tbsp
⅛ tsp	salt	⅛ tsp
	freshly ground black pepper	
150 g	low-fat ricotta	5 oz
3 tbsp	freshly grated Parmesan cheese	3 tbsp
1 tbsp	cornmeal	1 tbsp
½ tbsp	safflower oil	½ tbsp
Dough		
7 g	dried yeast	¼ oz
¼ tsp	sugar	¼ tsp
300 to 325 g	strong plain flour	10 to 11 oz
¼ tsp	salt	¼ tsp
3 tbsp	virgin olive oil	3 tbsp

Begin by making the dough. Pour ¼ litre (8 fl oz) of lukewarm water into a bowl, then sprinkle the yeast and sugar into it. After 2 or 3 minutes, stir to dissolve them thoroughly. Leave the bowl in a warm place until the yeast bubbles up — about 10 minutes.

Sift the flour and ¼ teaspoon of salt into a large bowl. Make a well in the centre and pour into it the yeast mixture and the olive oil. Mix the dough by hand; it should feel slightly sticky. If necessary, add a little more water or, if the mixture sticks to your hands, work in as much as 30 g (1 oz) additional flour, a tablespoon at a time, until the dough can be gathered into a ball. Place the ball of dough on a floured board and knead it until it is smooth and elastic — about 10 minutes.

Put the dough in an oiled bowl, turn the dough once to coat it with the oil, and cover it with a damp cloth. Set the bowl in a warm, draught-free place until the dough has doubled in bulk — about 1½ hours.

While the dough is rising, prepare the filling. In a large saucepan, combine the tomatoes, red onions, carrots, vinegar, garlic, sage, salt and pepper. Cook the mixture over high heat for 10 minutes, stirring occasionally. Reduce the heat to medium and cook until the liquid has evaporated — about 20 minutes more. (A fairly dry filling ensures crisp dough.) Set the mixture aside; do not refrigerate it.

Meanwhile, pour enough water into a large sauce-pan to fill it 2.5 cm (1 inch) deep. Bring the water to the boil. Add the kale, cover the pan, and cook for 8 minutes, stirring once. Drain the kale, refresh it under cold running water, then squeeze it by hand into a ball to rid it of excess moisture. Slice the ball at 5 mm (¼ inch) intervals, then put the kale in a large bowl. Add the ricotta, the Parmesan cheese and a dash of pepper, and mix well. Set aside at room temperature.

Preheat the oven to 230°C (450°F or Mark 8). When the dough has doubled, knock it down, then divide it into four equal portions. With your fingers, press each piece of dough into a 15 cm (6 inch) circle. Slightly off-centre on each round of dough, place a quarter of the kale mixture. Top each portion with a quarter of the tomato sauce, leaving a 1 cm (½ inch) border of the dough uncovered.

Fold each round of dough in half over the filling; then pinch the edges of the dough together, sealing the filling inside. Scatter the cornmeal on a heavy baking sheet, then arrange the calzones on it and brush them with the safflower oil. Bake the calzones until they are golden-brown — 18 to 20 minutes. Serve hot.

EDITOR'S NOTE: *To make the calzone dough with a food processor, mix 300 g (10 oz) of the flour and ¼ teaspoon of salt in the processor with two short bursts. In a separate small bowl, combine the yeast mixture (after it has bubbled up) with 3 tablespoons of olive oil. While the motor is running, pour the liquid into the processor as fast as the flour will absorb it; process until a ball of dough comes away from the sides of the bowl — about 1 minute. If the dough is too sticky to form a ball, add up to 30 g (1 oz) of additional flour, 1 tablespoon at a time. Remove the dough from the processor, place it on a floured board and knead it for 5 minutes. Set the dough aside to rise as described above.*

Kale Gratin with Ricotta and Parmesan Cheese

Serves 10
Working time: about 40 minutes
Total time: about 1 hour and 15 minutes

Calories **130**
Protein **7g**
Cholesterol **5mg**
Total fat **4g**
Saturated fat **1g**
Sodium **165mg**

1.5 kg	kale, washed, stems removed	3 lb
¼ litre	unsalted chicken or vegetable stock	8 fl oz
1	onion, chopped	1
90 g	long-grain rice	3 oz
1 tbsp	chopped fresh thyme, or 1 tsp dried thyme	1 tbsp
125 g	low-fat ricotta	4 oz
5 tbsp	freshly grated Parmesan cheese	5 tbsp
¼ tsp	grated nutmeg	¼ tsp
¼ tsp	salt	¼ tsp
	freshly ground black pepper	
15 g	fresh white breadcrumbs	½ oz
1 tbsp	virgin olive oil	1 tbsp

Pour the stock into a small saucepan, add the onion and bring the liquid to the boil over high heat. Add the rice and thyme. Reduce the heat to medium low, cover the pan, and simmer the rice until it is tender — about 15 minutes.

Preheat the oven to 200°C (400°F or Mark 6).

Meanwhile, put the kale in a large saucepan, cover the pan tightly and cook the kale over medium-high heat until it wilts — 3 to 4 minutes. (The water clinging to the leaves provides enough moisture.) Drain the kale and coarsely chop it. Combine the kale with the rice, ricotta, 4 tablespoons of the Parmesan cheese, the nutmeg, salt and pepper.

Put the mixture into a lightly oiled 1½ litre (2½ pint) gratin dish. Sprinkle on the breadcrumbs and the

remaining Parmesan cheese. Dribble the olive oil over the top and bake in the upper third of the oven until the juices begin bubbling — about 30 minutes. Remove the gratin from the oven and turn on the grill. Place the gratin under the grill to brown — about 5 minutes. Serve immediately.

Stewed Kale with Sweet Potatoes

Serves 6
Working time: about 20 minutes
Total time: about 45 minutes

Calories **170**
Protein **7g**
Cholesterol **5mg**
Total fat **2g**
Saturated fat **0g**
Sodium **155mg**

1 kg	kale, washed, stems removed	2 lb
500 g	sweet potatoes, peeled and diced	1 lb
1	small onion, finely chopped	1
2	garlic cloves, finely chopped	2
½ litre	unsalted chicken or vegetable stock	16 fl oz
⅛ tsp	grated nutmeg	⅛ tsp
¼ tsp	salt	¼ tsp
	freshly ground black pepper	

Put the kale in a large, heavy pan, cover the pan and cook the kale over medium-high heat until it wilts — about 3 to 4 minutes. (The water clinging to the leaves provides enough moisture.) Add the remaining ingredients, stir together well, and partially cover the pan so that a little steam can escape. Stew the vegetables over medium-high heat, stirring occasionally, until the liquid has nearly evaporated — about 25 minutes. Transfer to a vegetable dish and serve.

Vegetable-Stuffed Cos Rolls

Serves 6
Working time: about 1 hour
Total time: about 1 hour and 10 minutes

Calories **95**
Protein **4g**
Cholesterol **0mg**
Total fat **5g**
Saturated fat **1g**
Sodium **150mg**

12	large cos lettuce leaves	12
1	cucumber, peeled, halved lengthwise, seeded and shredded into long strips	1
1 tsp	low-sodium soy sauce, or naturally fermented shoyu	1 tsp
¼ litre	unsalted chicken or vegetable stock	8 fl oz
1 tbsp	safflower oil	1 tbsp
2	carrots, peeled and shredded into long strips	2
500 g	yellow squash or courgettes, halved lengthwise, seeded and shredded into long strips	1 lb
8	spring onions, green tops removed, white bottoms thinly sliced lengthwise	8
1	garlic clove, finely chopped	1
¼ tsp	salt	¼ tsp
	freshly ground black pepper	
150 g	shelled peas, blanched for 1 minute and drained, or thawed frozen peas	5 oz
1 tbsp	dark sesame oil	1 tbsp

Put the cucumber in a bowl and toss it with the soy sauce. Set the cucumber aside to marinate. Place the lettuce leaves in a large saucepan and pour 12.5 cl (4 fl oz) of the stock over them. Place foil directly over the leaves and cover the pan. Bring the stock to the boil, reduce the heat to medium low, and steam the leaves until wilted — about 7 minutes. Drain them on paper towels.

With your hands, squeeze the liquid from the cucumber. In a heavy frying pan, heat the safflower oil over high heat. Add the carrots and sauté them, stirring constantly, for 1 minute. Add the cucumber, squash,

spring onions, garlic, salt and pepper; sauté, stirring constantly, for 5 minutes more. Transfer the mixture to a bowl and stir in the peas and sesame oil.

Cut out the thickest part of the stem in a V shape from the base of each leaf. Overlap the cut edges, then roll up the mixture in the leaves as shown below.

Pour the remaining 12.5 cl (4 fl oz) of stock into a large frying pan. Arrange the cos rolls in the frying pan, with their seam sides down; cover the pan and cook the rolls over low heat until they are heated through — about 10 minutes. Remove the rolls from the pan with a slotted spoon and serve them immediately.

Stuffing and Rolling a Vegetable Leaf

Rolling up a prepared stuffing in individual vegetable leaves makes for an attractive — and surprisingly simple — presentation.

After rinsing and cooking the leaves as called for in the recipe, gently blot each one dry with a paper towel. For a cos lettuce leaf, cut out the thickest part of the leaf's centre rib in an elongated V — 5 to 10 cm (2 to 4 inches) in length, depending on the size of the leaf — and overlap the two cut edges to close the cut. To make a large cabbage leaf easier to roll, use a knife to shave about half the thickness from the protruding ridge of its centre rib. Preserved vine leaves need only be trimmed of their hard stem, if one is present. The leaves may then be stuffed and rolled, following the technique on the right.

1 ADDING THE STUFFING. Place stuffing in an oblong mound above the leaf's base. Fold the base over the stuffing, then fold both long edges over the ends of the stuffing to encase it snugly.

2 ROLLING UP THE LEAF. Gently roll the stuffing mound towards the leaf tip, tucking in the edges if they loosen, to form a compact roll. Repeat these steps with the remaining leaves and stuffing.

Parsley with Burghul and Orange

Serves 6
Working time: about 45 minutes
Total time: about 1 hour

Calories **140**
Protein **4g**
Cholesterol **0mg**
Total fat **5g**
Saturated fat **0g**
Sodium **70mg**

225 g	parsley leaves	7½ oz
2 tbsp	safflower oil	2 tbsp
90 g	finely chopped onion	3 oz
90 g	burghul	3 oz
⅛ tsp	salt	⅛ tsp
17.5 cl	fresh orange juice	6 fl oz
60 g	grated radish	2 oz
	freshly ground black pepper	
3 tbsp	rice vinegar	3 tbsp
1	orange, peeled and segmented, the pith and membrane removed	1

Heat 1 tablespoon of the oil in a saucepan over medium heat. Add the onion and cook it, stirring once, for 2 minutes. Add the burghul and cook the mixture, stirring frequently, for 5 minutes more.

Stir in the salt, orange juice and 6 cl (2 fl oz) of water, and raise the heat to medium high. When the mixture starts to simmer, reduce the heat to low; partially cover the pan, leaving a 2.5 cm (1 inch) opening to vent the steam. Cook, stirring occasionally, until the burghul has absorbed all the liquid — 15 to 20 minutes. Transfer the burghul mixture to a bowl, fluff it up with a fork, and refrigerate it.

While the burghul is cooking, pour enough water into a saucepan to fill it about 2.5 cm (1 inch) deep. Set a vegetable steamer in the pan and bring the water to the boil. Put the parsley in the steamer, cover the pan tightly, and steam the parsley until it turns a brighter green and is

partially wilted — about 3 minutes. Immediately transfer the parsley to a large bowl and refrigerate it.

When the burghul and the parsley have cooled, combine them. Then add the radish and the pepper, and toss well. In a small bowl, whisk together the remaining oil and the vinegar; dribble this liquid over the parsley and burghul. Add the orange segments and toss lightly. Transfer the mixture to a serving dish and serve it cool.

Calories **140**
Protein **7g**
Cholesterol **5mg**
Total fat **6g**
Saturated fat **1g**
Sodium **45mg**

Parsley and Chick-Pea Patties with Yogurt Sauce

Serves 6
Working time: about 20 minutes
Total time: about 2 hours and 30 minutes

25 g	parsley leaves	¾ oz
100 g	dried chick-peas	3½ oz
3	spring onions, trimmed and chopped	3
10 g	fresh mint, or 1 tbsp dried mint	⅓ oz
1	small leek, trimmed, cleaned (page 110) and chopped	1
1	garlic clove, chopped	1
¼ tsp	ground cumin	¼ tsp
¼ tsp	ground coriander	¼ tsp
⅛ tsp	ground cardamom (optional)	⅛ tsp
1	egg white	1
1	lemon, juice strained	1
125 g	finely shredded cos lettuce leaves	4 oz
2 tbsp	virgin olive oil	2 tbsp
¼ litre	plain low-fat yogurt	8 fl oz

Put the chick-peas in a saucepan and pour in enough water to cover them. Bring the water to the boil and remove the pan from the heat. Let the chick-peas soak for at least 1 hour. Return the chick-peas to the boil, reduce the heat, and simmer until they are tender — about 1 hour.

Drain the chick-peas and place them in a food processor or blender. Add the parsley, spring onions, mint, leek, garlic, cumin, coriander, cardamom, egg white and half of the lemon juice. Purée the chick-pea mixture until it becomes a smooth paste — 3 to 4 minutes. Roll the paste into 12 walnut-sized balls and flatten each one with the palm of your hand.

Scatter the lettuce over the bottom of a serving dish. Heat 1 tablespoon of the olive oil in a large, heavy frying pan over medium-high heat, using a pastry brush to distribute the oil evenly in the pan. Cook half of the patties for 2 minutes on each side and arrange them on the lettuce bed. Cook the second batch of patties in the remaining tablespoon of oil and arrange them on the lettuce bed as well.

Mix the yogurt with the remaining lemon juice. Pour a little of this sauce over each patty, and pass the rest of the sauce separately.

Vine Leaves Stuffed with Couscous

Serves 6
Working time: about 45 minutes
Total time: about 1 hour and 15 minutes

Calories **160**
Protein **8g**
Cholesterol **10mg**
Total fat **7g**
Saturated fat **1g**
Sodium **145mg**

18	fresh vine leaves, cooked 5 minutes in boiling water and refreshed under cold running water, or preserved vine leaves, rinsed	18
175 g	couscous	6 oz
500 g	mushrooms, wiped clean, finely chopped	1 lb
2	lemons, juice only	2
1	small onion, finely chopped	1
3	spring onions, chopped	3
1 tbsp	chopped fresh thyme, or 1 tsp dried thyme	1 tbsp
30 g	toasted almonds, chopped	1 oz
1 tbsp	virgin olive oil	1 tbsp
¼ tsp	salt	¼ tsp
	freshly ground black pepper	
½ litre	unsalted chicken or vegetable stock	16 fl oz
1	lemon, sliced	1

Place the couscous in a bowl and pour 30 cl (½ pint) of boiling water over it. Stir with a fork and let stand until the water is absorbed — about 10 minutes.

Place the mushrooms, half the lemon juice, the onion, spring onions and thyme in a saucepan; pour in enough water to cover. Bring the mixture to the boil over high heat, then reduce the heat to medium low and simmer for 10 minutes. Drain the mushrooms and discard the liquid. Preheat the oven to 200°C (400°F or Mark 6).

Combine the couscous, the mushroom mixture, almonds, oil, salt and pepper. Put a generous tablespoonful of filling close to the stem end of each leaf. Roll up the leaves, tucking in the edges to keep the cous-

cous from spilling out *(leaf-rolling technique, page 51)*, and pack them seam side down into a baking dish. Pour the stock into the dish and dribble the remaining lemon juice over the stuffed leaves. Cover tightly with aluminium foil and bake for 30 minutes. The stuffed leaves may be served warm or cold. Garnish the dish with the lemon slices just before serving.

Steamed Spinach with Water Chestnuts

Serves 6
Working time: about 20 minutes
Total time: about 30 minutes

Calories **65**
Protein **6g**
Cholesterol **0mg**
Total fat **2g**
Saturated fat **0g**
Sodium **295mg**

1 kg	spinach, washed, stems removed	2 lb
¼ tsp	Sichuan peppercorns, or ⅛ tsp freshly ground black pepper	¼ tsp
2 tbsp	low-sodium soy sauce, or naturally fermented shoyu	2 tbsp
1½ tsp	safflower oil	1½ tsp
½ tsp	dark sesame oil	½ tsp
1 tbsp	rice vinegar or cider vinegar	1 tbsp
¼ tsp	sugar	¼ tsp
125 g	water chestnuts, halved	4 oz

In a small, heavy frying pan, toast the peppercorns over medium heat for 3 minutes, shaking the pan frequently. Transfer the peppercorns to a work surface and crush them. In a small bowl, combine the soy sauce, oils, vinegar, pepper and sugar.

Place the spinach in a large pan, cover, and steam it over medium-high heat until it is wilted — about 2 minutes. (The water clinging to the leaves provides enough moisture.) Drain the spinach thoroughly and put it back in the pan. Stir in the water chestnuts and the soy sauce mixture, bring the liquid to the boil, and cook the spinach for 3 minutes. Transfer to a vegetable dish and serve.

Sautéed Spinach and Spiced Potatoes

Serves 4
Working time: about 30 minutes
Total time: about 45 minutes

Calories **100**
Protein **3g**
Cholesterol **0mg**
Total fat **4g**
Saturated fat **0g**
Sodium **160mg**

500 g	spinach, washed, stems removed	1 lb
250 g	potatoes, peeled and cut into 1 cm (½ inch) cubes	8 oz
½ tsp	salt	½ tsp
1 tbsp	safflower oil	1 tbsp
90 g	onion, finely chopped	3 oz
1	garlic clove, finely chopped	1
1 tsp	paprika	1 tsp
⅛ tsp	cayenne pepper	⅛ tsp
	freshly ground black pepper	
1 tsp	red wine vinegar	1 tsp

Place the washed spinach, with water still clinging to the leaves, in a large saucepan. Put on the lid, and steam the spinach over medium heat until wilted — 2 to 3 minutes. Chop the spinach coarsely and set aside.

Place the potato cubes in a saucepan and add enough water to cover them. Add ¼ teaspoon of the salt and bring the liquid to the boil, then reduce the heat to medium low. Cook the potatoes until they are soft but not crumbly — 5 to 7 minutes. Drain the potatoes and then put them on paper towels to soak up the excess liquid.

In a large, heavy frying pan, heat the oil over medium-high heat. Add the potato cubes and sauté them, stirring frequently, until they are browned — about 5 minutes. Add the onion and cook, stirring occasionally, for 2 minutes more. Stir in the garlic and then sprinkle the potatoes with the paprika, cayenne pepper and black pepper. Toss the mixture to coat the potatoes. Add the spinach and cook until it is warmed through — about 1 minute. Stir in the vinegar and the remaining salt, and serve immediately.

EDITOR'S NOTE: *Waxy potatoes, rather than floury ones, are preferred for this recipe.*

3 Amid artful representations of vegetables in this section, baked aubergine halves stuffed with spiced potato, carrot and courgette stand ready for serving.

A Fruitful Abundance

Vegetables can be fruits. The tomato is one, and so are the aubergines, beans, cucumbers, peppers and squashes that help to fill this chapter with cornucopian abundance. The main difference between them and apples or pears is that fruit vegetables are not customarily considered sweet; but, like apples and pears, they are the seed-bearing "packets" of the plant on which they grow. In some instances, of course, it is the seed rather than the packet that is eaten, as with peas, broad beans, sweetcorn and the other pod and seed vegetables covered in this section.

Of fruit vegetables, the tomato is far and away the most popular, eaten not just fresh, but in so many different dishes (especially in sauces) that it may provide many people with more nutritional value than they derive from any other vegetable. One medium, raw tomato provides almost all of the Recommended Daily Amount of vitamin C and close to a quarter of the RDA of vitamin A, but only about 20 calories.

Many of the fruit, pod and seed vegetables are fragile. Most tomatoes are transported unripe to market to protect them from damage. Unless sweet, juicy, freshly picked tomatoes are available, for some recipes you may wish to use canned tomatoes or to buy tomatoes at the supermarket three or four days in advance of use and allow them to ripen at home. This is best accomplished by putting them in a paper bag or covering them with a cloth, and leaving them at room temperature away from sunlight. The addition of an apple to the bag will actually hasten the process, thanks to the ethylene gas the apple emits.

While tomatoes can go on ripening at home, fresh peas and sweetcorn lose sweetness as their sugars begin to turn to starch. The way around this dilemma is to refrigerate them as quickly as possible: the cold temperature will slow down starch production. Sweetcorn stored at 0°C (32°F) will retain much of its sugar, but left at room temperature it will lose almost half its sugar in a day. Fortunately, the kernels of some of today's varieties are sweeter than ever.

Fruit, pod and seed vegetables vary widely in nutritive value. Cucumbers and aubergines have almost none, especially when peeled; but they are low in sodium and calories, and they are good sources of fibre. Sweet peppers, on the other hand, have more vitamin C than tomatoes; indeed, they contain half as much again as oranges. Broad beans and peas offer good protein. The summer squashes — courgettes, chayotes and custard marrows — are a source of vitamin C, while orange-fleshed winter squashes such as pumpkin are sources of vitamin A. The squashes are low in calories, too; 100 g (3 oz) of cooked courgettes has just 16 calories.

Sautéed French Beans with Radishes and Fennel Seed

Serves 6
Working time: about 20 minutes
Total time: about 30 minutes

Calories **60**
Protein **1g**
Cholesterol **5mg**
Total fat **5g**
Saturated fat **2g**
Sodium **95mg**

500 g	French beans, topped and tailed	1 lb
1 tbsp	virgin olive oil	1 tbsp
1 tbsp	unsalted butter	1 tbsp
2 tsp	fennel seeds	2 tsp
125 g	radishes, trimmed and sliced into 3 mm (⅛ inch) rounds	4 oz
3	spring onions, trimmed, thinly sliced	3
¼ tsp	salt	¼ tsp
	freshly ground black pepper	
1 tbsp	fresh lime or lemon juice	1 tbsp

In a large saucepan, bring 2 litres (3½ pints) of water to a rapid boil. Add the beans and, after the water returns to the boil, cook them for 4 minutes. Remove them from the pan and refresh them under cold running water to preserve their colour. Drain the beans and set aside.

In a large, heavy frying pan, heat the oil and butter over medium-high heat. When the butter has melted, add the beans and the fennel seeds. Sauté for 3 minutes, stirring frequently. Add the radishes, spring onions, salt, pepper, and lime or lemon juice. Sauté, stirring constantly, until the beans are tender but crisp — about 3 minutes more. Serve immediately.

Chilled Beans with Yogurt and Mint

Serves 6
Working time: about 20 minutes
Total time: about 50 minutes

Calories **40**
Protein **2g**
Cholesterol **0mg**
Total fat **1g**
Saturated fat **0g**
Sodium **100mg**

500 g	French beans, topped and tailed	1 lb
¼ tsp	salt	¼ tsp
1½ tsp	dry mustard	1½ tsp
1 tbsp	fresh lime or lemon juice	1 tbsp
2 tbsp	chopped fresh mint	2 tbsp
1	small garlic clove, very finely chopped	1
½ tsp	sugar	½ tsp
	freshly ground black pepper	
8 cl	plain low-fat yogurt	3 fl oz
1	tomato, cut into wedges	1

Pour enough water into a large saucepan to fill it about 2.5 cm (1 inch) deep. Set a vegetable steamer in the pan and bring the water to the boil. Add the beans, cover the pan tightly, and steam the beans until they are tender — about 6 minutes. Remove the beans from the pan, and refresh them under cold running water to arrest their cooking and preserve their colour. When the beans are cool, drain them thoroughly and place them in a bowl. Sprinkle the salt over the beans and toss well.

In a bowl, stir together the dry mustard and the lime or lemon juice until a smooth paste is formed. Add the mint, garlic, sugar, pepper and yogurt, and blend well. Add the beans and toss to coat them. Refrigerate for at least 30 minutes. At serving time, garnish with the tomato wedges.

Stir-Fried French Beans with Fermented Black Beans

Serves 6
Working time: about 15 minutes
Total time: about 20 minutes

Calories **55**
Protein **2g**
Cholesterol **0mg**
Total fat **3g**
Saturated fat **0g**
Sodium **245mg**

500 g	French beans, topped and tailed	1 lb
½	lime or lemon	½
1 tbsp	safflower oil	1 tbsp
1 tsp	cornflour mixed with 1 tbsp low-sodium soy sauce, or naturally fermented shoyu, and 6 cl (2 fl oz) water	1 tsp
2 tbsp	fermented black beans, rinsed	2 tbsp
	freshly ground black pepper	

Bring 2 litres (3½ pints) of water to the boil in a saucepan. Squeeze the lime or lemon juice into the water, then drop in the rind. Plunge the green beans into the water and cook them for 4 minutes after the water comes back to the boil — they should still be crisp. Drain the beans and refresh them under cold running water until they are cool. Discard the lime or lemon rind.

Heat the oil in a wok or heavy frying pan over high heat. Sauté the green beans, stirring constantly, until they are tender — about 3 minutes. Turn down the heat to medium and cook 1 minute more. Stir the cornflour mixture and the black beans together. Pour this mixture on to the French beans, sprinkle with the pepper and stir well. Continue cooking for 1 minute more and transfer to a serving dish. Serve the beans immediately.

EDITOR'S NOTE: *The fermented black beans called for in this recipe are available where Asian foods are sold.*

Broad Beans with Horseradish and Tomato

Serves 4
Working (and total) time: about 20 minutes

Calories **150**
Protein **8g**
Cholesterol **0mg**
Total fat **3g**
Saturated fat **0g**
Sodium **140mg**

300 g	fresh shelled, or frozen, broad beans	10 oz
2 tsp	safflower oil	2 tsp
¼ tsp	salt	¼ tsp
	freshly ground black pepper	
2 tsp	horseradish	2 tsp
1	small tomato, skinned, seeded (page 84) and coarsely chopped	1
2 tbsp	finely chopped fresh coriander	2 tbsp

Bring 1 litre (1¾ pints) of water to the boil in a saucepan. Cook the beans in the water until barely tender — 8 to 10 minutes — then drain them and set them aside. (If you ▶

are using frozen beans, cook them in 6 cl/2 fl oz of boiling water for 6 to 10 minutes.)

In a large, heavy frying pan, heat the oil over medium-high heat. Add the beans and sauté them, stirring frequently, for 2 minutes. Sprinkle the beans with the salt and pepper. Stir in the horseradish and tomato, and sauté, stirring constantly, for 1 minute more. Transfer the mixture to a serving dish, sprinkle with the coriander and serve immediately.

Wax Beans and Cherry Tomatoes

Serves 6
Working time: about 25 minutes
Total time: about 30 minutes

Calories **70**
Protein **2g**
Cholesterol **0mg**
Total fat **5g**
Saturated fat **1g**
Sodium **95mg**

500 g	wax beans, topped and tailed	1 lb
2 tbsp	virgin olive oil	2 tbsp
1	small onion, thinly sliced	1
1	garlic clove, finely chopped	1
6	cherry tomatoes, halved	6
2 tbsp	chopped fresh basil, plus several whole leaves for garnish	2 tbsp
¼ tsp	salt	¼ tsp
	freshly ground black pepper	

Pour enough water into a saucepan to fill it about 2.5 cm (1 inch) deep. Set a vegetable steamer in the pan and bring the water to the boil. Put the beans in the steamer, cover the pan, and steam the beans until they are tender but still crisp — 5 to 7 minutes.

Pour the oil into a large frying pan over medium heat. Cook the onion and garlic in the oil until the onions are soft — 2 to 3 minutes. Add the beans and cook, stirring from time to time, for 2 minutes. Add the tomatoes, chopped basil, salt and pepper. Stir well and continue cooking until the tomatoes are heated through — about 2 minutes. Transfer the vegetables to a serving dish and garnish them with the whole basil leaves. Serve immediately.

Sweetcorn and Red Pepper Pancakes

Serves 8
Working time: about 30 minutes
Total time: about 45 minutes

Calories **110**
Protein **4g**
Cholesterol **35mg**
Total fat **5g**
Saturated fat **1g**
Sodium **160mg**

325 g	fresh sweetcorn kernels (about 2 large ears), or frozen sweetcorn, thawed	11 oz
1	egg yolk	1
30 g	cornmeal	1 oz
30 g	flour	1 oz
1 tsp	fresh thyme, or ¼ tsp dried thyme	1 tsp
½ tsp	salt	½ tsp
	freshly ground black pepper	
150 g	sweet red pepper, seeded, deribbed, and finely chopped	5 oz
4	egg whites	4
8 tsp	virgin olive oil	8 tsp

Chop half of the sweetcorn finely, by hand or in a blender. Place in a large bowl. Add the egg yolk, cornmeal, flour, thyme, salt and pepper to the bowl, and stir well. Add the sweet red pepper and the remaining kernels, and mix to incorporate them. Set this mixture aside.

In another bowl, beat the egg whites until soft peaks form. Fold half of the egg whites into the sweetcorn and red pepper mixture, and blend well. Then carefully fold in the remaining egg whites; the whites should not be completely incorporated.

Heat a large, heavy frying pan (preferably one with a non-stick surface) over medium heat. Put 2 teaspoons of the oil in the pan. When the oil is hot, drop tablespoonfuls of the sweetcorn and red pepper mixture into the pan, taking care not to let the edges touch. Cook until the bottom side of each pancake is golden-brown — about 3 minutes. Turn the pancakes carefully and cook them until the other side browns — about 3 minutes more. Remove the finished pancakes from the pan and keep them warm. Repeat the process, using 2 teaspoons of the oil each time, until all of the batter has been used. Serve immediately.

EDITOR'S NOTE: *If you are using frozen sweetcorn, whisk 1 teaspoon of sugar into the egg yolk.*

Sautéed Cucumbers with Red Leaf Lettuce and Dill

Serves 4
Working (and total) time: about 20 minutes

Calories **55**
Protein **1g**
Cholesterol **15mg**
Total fat **5g**
Saturated fat **3g**
Sodium **140mg**

750 g	cucumbers, peeled, halved, seeded and sliced into 5 mm (¼ inch) pieces	1½ lb
15 g	unsalted butter	½ oz
2	shallots, finely chopped	2
¼ tsp	salt	¼ tsp
	white pepper	
4	leaves red or oak leaf lettuce, torn into large pieces	4
10 g	fresh dill, coarsely chopped	⅓ oz
1 tbsp	double cream	1 tbsp
	freshly ground black pepper	

In a large, heavy frying pan, melt the butter over medium-high heat. Add the shallots and sauté them, stirring constantly, until they turn translucent — about 1 minute. Stir in the cucumbers, sprinkle with the salt and white pepper, and cook them until they are slightly limp — about 3 minutes more. Add the lettuce and dill, and cook until the lettuce has wilted — about 1 minute. Pour in the cream and allow it to heat through — about 1 minute more. Sprinkle the vegetables with black pepper and serve immediately.

Cucumber Mousse
with Gazpacho Sauce

Serves 8
Working time: about 45 minutes
Total time: about 2 hours and 30 minutes

Calories **70**
Protein **5g**
Cholesterol **5mg**
Total fat **3g**
Saturated fat **1g**
Sodium **50mg**

500 g	cucumbers, peeled, seeded and cut into 5 cm (2 inch) strips	1 lb
2 tbsp	powdered gelatine	2 tbsp
17.5 cl	unsalted chicken or vegetable stock	6 fl oz
¼ litre	plain low-fat yogurt	8 fl oz
1	lime, juice only	1
6	drops Tabasco sauce	6
2	spring onions, white bottoms chopped, green tops finely chopped and reserved for the sauce	2
1	hot green chili pepper, seeded (caution, page 106)	1
1 tbsp	chopped fresh coriander	1 tbsp
Gazpacho sauce		
1 kg	tomatoes, skinned, seeded (page 84) and finely chopped	2 lb
1 tbsp	virgin olive oil	1 tbsp
1	lime, juice only	1
4	drops Tabasco sauce	4
1	garlic clove, very finely chopped	1
1 tbsp	chopped fresh coriander	1 tbsp

In a small bowl, soften the gelatine in 6 cl (2 fl oz) of the stock until it is spongy. In a small saucepan, bring the remaining stock to the boil. Add the gelatine mixture to the stock and stir to dissolve the gelatine thoroughly. Set the gelatine mixture aside.

Purée the cucumbers, yogurt, lime juice, Tabasco sauce, spring onion bottoms, chili pepper and coriander in a food processor or blender. Add the gelatine mixture ▶

and blend. Pour the mixture into a 2 litre (3½ pint) mould and chill until firm — at least 2 hours.

To make the sauce, mix the tomatoes, oil, lime juice, Tabasco sauce, garlic, reserved spring onion tops and coriander in a bowl. Refrigerate the sauce.

At serving time, run a blade along the edge of the mould to loosen the mousse. Set the mould in shallow hot water for 30 seconds, then invert the mousse on to a serving platter. Spoon the sauce around the mousse.

Aubergine Parmesan with Mint

Serves 8
Working time: about 20 minutes
Total time: about 1 hour and 45 minutes

Calories **65**
Protein **4g**
Cholesterol **5mg**
Total fat **4g**
Saturated fat **1g**
Sodium **210mg**

500 g	aubergines, cut into 1 cm (½ inch) cubes	1 lb
½ tsp	salt	½ tsp
2	tomatoes, skinned, seeded (page 84) and chopped	2
1	garlic clove, finely chopped	1
1 tbsp	chopped fresh mint leaves	1 tbsp
1 tbsp	virgin olive oil	1 tbsp
60 g	low-fat mozzarella, freshly grated	2 oz
3 tbsp	freshly grated Parmesan cheese	3 tbsp

In a bowl, toss the aubergine with the salt. Place the aubergine in a colander, and weigh it down with a plate small enough to rest on top of the cubes. Let the aubergine drain for 30 minutes to eliminate its natural bitterness. Rinse the aubergine under cold running water to rid it of the salt, and drain it well.

Preheat the oven to 200°C (400°F or Mark 6). In a 23 by 33 cm (9 by 13 inch) rectangular baking dish, mix together the aubergine, tomatoes, garlic, mint and oil. Cover the dish with aluminium foil and bake until the aubergine is very tender — about 1 hour. Remove the dish from the oven and sprinkle the grated cheeses over the top. Re-cover the dish and bake until the cheeses have melted — about 5 minutes more. Serve immediately.

Aubergine Shells Stuffed with Spiced Vegetables

Serves 4
Working time: about 30 minutes
Total time: about 1 hour and 10 minutes

Calories **85**
Protein **4g**
Cholesterol **0mg**
Total fat **1g**
Saturated fat **0g**
Sodium **25mg**

1	large aubergine (about 500 g/1 lb), halved lengthwise	1
1	medium potato, peeled and cut into 5 mm (¼ inch) cubes	1
1	carrot, peeled and cut into 5 mm (¼ inch) cubes	1
1	medium courgette, cut into 5 mm (¼ inch) cubes	1
12.5 cl	unsalted chicken or vegetable stock	4 fl oz
1	small onion, thinly sliced	1
⅛ tsp	ground cumin	⅛ tsp
Indian spice mixture		
¼ tsp	ground cumin	¼ tsp
¼ tsp	turmeric	¼ tsp
¼ tsp	ground cardamom	¼ tsp
¼ tsp	ground coriander	¼ tsp
⅛ tsp	ground cloves	⅛ tsp
⅛ tsp	ground mace	⅛ tsp
⅛ tsp	cayenne pepper	⅛ tsp
⅛ tsp	cinnamon	⅛ tsp

In a bowl, combine all the ingredients for the spice mixture. Set the mixture aside.

Pour enough water into a large saucepan to fill it 2.5 cm (1 inch) deep. Set a steamer in the pan and bring the water to the boil. Put the potato and carrot cubes in the steamer, cover the pan, and steam the vegetables for 2 minutes. Add the courgette and steam until all the vegetables are tender — about 3 minutes more. Empty the contents of the steamer into a bowl and set the bowl aside. Return the steamer to the pan.

With a small knife, cut around the perimeter of an aubergine half, leaving a 5 mm (¼ inch) wall all round. Then slice deep into the flesh in a crisscross pattern. Care-

fully remove the cut segments with a spoon. Repeat the process with the other aubergine half.

Place the aubergine shells in the steamer, skin side up. Cover the pan, return the water to the boil, and steam the shells until they are tender — about 5 minutes. Remove the shells and let them cool.

Preheat the oven to 190°C (375°F or Mark 5). In a second saucepan, bring the stock to the boil over medium-high heat. Add the spice mixture and the onion; cook, stirring occasionally, until the onion is translucent — about 3 minutes. Stir in the aubergine segments and cook until very soft — about 5 minutes more. Then stir in the potato, carrot and courgette cubes with the ⅛ teaspoon of cumin.

Spoon the vegetable mixture into the cooled aubergine shells and arrange the shells in a baking dish. Cover with aluminium foil and bake until the juices are bubbling — about 30 minutes. To serve, cut 1 cm (½ inch) off each shell's stem end, which may be tough. Then halve each shell lengthwise to make four portions.

Steamed Aubergine with Soy and Ginger

Serves 8
Working time: about 15 minutes
Total time: about 40 minutes

Calories **25**
Protein **2g**
Cholesterol **0mg**
Total fat **0g**
Saturated fat **0g**
Sodium **310mg**

4	aubergines (about 125 g/4 oz each), cut in half lengthwise	4
4 tbsp	low-sodium soy sauce, or naturally fermented shoyu	4 tbsp
2 tsp	dry sherry	2 tsp
1 tsp	molasses	1 tsp
¼ tsp	dark sesame oil	1 tsp
2 tsp	chopped fresh ginger root	2 tsp
2	garlic cloves, finely chopped	2
2	spring onions, cut diagonally into 2.5 cm (1 inch) long pieces, 3 mm (⅛ inch) thick	2

In a small bowl, combine the soy sauce, sherry, molasses, sesame oil, ginger and garlic. Set aside.

Score the skin of the aubergines with crisscross cuts 2.5 cm (1 inch) apart and 2 cm (¾ inch) deep. Place the halves, flat side down, on a heatproof plate, and pour the soy sauce mixture over them.

Pour enough water into a large saucepan to fill it 2.5 cm (1 inch) deep, place two small bowls on the bottom and rest the plate on top of them. Cover the pan, bring the water to the boil over high heat, and steam the aubergines until tender — about 10 minutes. Remove the plate, scatter the spring onions on the aubergine and allow the aubergine to come to room temperature before serving.

Mange-Tout in Basil Vinaigrette

Serves 8
Working time: about 15 minutes
Total time: about 20 minutes

Calories **115**
Protein **4g**
Cholesterol **0mg**
Total fat **7g**
Saturated fat **1g**
Sodium **70mg**

750 g	mange-tout, strings removed	1½ lb
1	shallot, finely chopped	1
2 tbsp	fresh lime juice	2 tbsp
2 tbsp	balsamic vinegar, or 1 tbsp red wine vinegar mixed with ½ tsp honey	2 tbsp
2 tbsp	safflower oil	2 tbsp
1 tbsp	olive oil	1 tbsp
1	garlic clove, finely chopped	1
1 tbsp	chopped fresh basil	1 tbsp
¼ tsp	salt	¼ tsp
	freshly ground black pepper	
30 g	whole almonds, toasted and chopped	1 oz

To prepare the basil vinaigrette, combine the lime juice and the balsamic vinegar in a small bowl. Steep the shallot in the mixture for 5 minutes. Whisk in the safflower and olive oils, garlic, basil, salt and pepper.

Bring 3 litres (5 pints) of water to the boil in a saucepan. Add the mange-tout to the rapidly boiling water, stir them once, and cook for 30 seconds only. Drain the mange-tout and refresh them under cold running water until they are cool. Drain the mange-tout again and toss them with the vinaigrette and almonds. Serve cold.

Green Peas with Curried Mushrooms

Serves 6
Working time: about 30 minutes
Total time: about 45 minutes

Calories **70**
Protein **5g**
Cholesterol **5mg**
Total fat **1g**
Saturated fat **0g**
Sodium **25mg**

1 kg	peas, shelled, or 300 g (10 oz) frozen peas, thawed	2 lb
12.5 cl	unsalted chicken or vegetable stock	4 fl oz
175 g	mushrooms, wiped clean, thinly sliced	6 oz
1	onion, chopped	1
1 tsp	curry powder	1 tsp
12.5 cl	plain low-fat yogurt	4 fl oz

If you are using fresh peas, parboil them until they are barely tender — 3 to 4 minutes. Drain the peas and refresh them under cold running water. Drain them again and set aside. (Frozen peas do not need to be parboiled.)

In a saucepan, bring the chicken stock to the boil. Add the mushrooms, onion and curry powder. Lower the heat to medium, and cook until almost no liquid remains — 10 to 15 minutes. Add the peas, and cook them until they are warmed through — about 5 minutes. Stir in the yogurt and remove the pan from the heat. Transfer the vegetables to a warmed serving dish and serve immediately.

Minted Green Peas with Cucumbers

Serves 6
Working time: about 30 minutes
Total time: about 45 minutes

Calories **45**
Protein **3g**
Cholesterol **0mg**
Total fat **0g**
Saturated fat **0g**
Sodium **95mg**

1 kg	peas, shelled, or 300 g (10 oz) frozen peas, thawed	2 lb
500 g	cucumbers	1 lb
12.5 cl	unsalted chicken or vegetable stock	4 fl oz
2 tbsp	finely chopped fresh mint, or 2 tsp dried mint	2 tbsp
¼ tsp	salt	¼ tsp
	freshly ground black pepper	

If you are using fresh peas, parboil them until they are barely tender — 3 to 4 minutes. Drain them, then refresh them under cold running water. Drain the peas again and set them aside. (Frozen peas do not need parboiling.)

Slice the cucumbers in half lengthwise, and remove the seeds with a spoon or a melon baller. Cut the cucumbers on the diagonal into 5 mm (¼ inch) slices. Bring a large saucepan of water to the boil and plunge the cucumbers in. Bring the water back to the boil and cook the cucumbers until they are barely tender — about 2 minutes. Drain them and set aside.

Bring the stock to the boil in a saucepan. Lower the heat to medium, and add the peas and cucumbers. Cook, stirring occasionally, until both vegetables are heated through — about 5 minutes. Stir in the mint, salt and pepper. Transfer the vegetables to a warmed vegetable dish and serve immediately.

Sugar Snap Peas and Red Grapes

Serves 4
Working (and total) time: about 25 minutes

Calories **80**
Protein **3g**
Cholesterol **5mg**
Total fat **3g**
Saturated fat **2g**
Sodium **135mg**

350 g	sugar snap peas, strings and stems removed	12 oz
15 g	unsalted butter	½ oz
1	shallot, finely chopped	1
¼ tsp	salt	¼ tsp
	freshly ground black pepper	
90 g	seedless red grapes, halved lengthwise	3 oz
1 tbsp	dry white wine	1 tbsp

Blanch the peas in boiling water for 2 minutes. Drain the peas, then refresh them under cold running water until cool. Drain them again and set them aside.

Heat the butter in a heavy frying pan over medium heat. Cook the shallot until soft — about 2 minutes. Add the peas, salt and pepper, and cook until the peas are heated through — 2 to 3 minutes. Add the grapes and wine, and cook until the wine has evaporated — about 1 minute. Serve immediately.

EDITOR'S NOTE: *Mange-tout work equally well in this recipe. Blanch them for 30 seconds only.*

Sweet Pepper Sauté with Courgettes

Serves 6
Working time: about 35 minutes
Total time: about 40 minutes

Calories **40**
Protein **1g**
Cholesterol **0mg**
Total fat **2g**
Saturated fat **0g**
Sodium **5mg**

3	small sweet peppers, (one red, one green, one yellow) seeded, deribbed and cut into 2.5 cm (1 inch) squares	3
1	onion, coarsely chopped	1
6	garlic cloves, finely chopped	6
¼ tsp	crushed fennel seeds	¼ tsp
1 tbsp	virgin olive oil	1 tbsp
250 g	courgettes, trimmed and cut into 2.5 cm (1 inch) cubes	8 oz
⅛ tsp	saffron threads, soaked in 2 tbsp water	⅛ tsp
1 tbsp	anise-flavoured liqueur (optional)	1 tbsp
4 tbsp	chopped fresh basil, or 4 tbsp chopped parsley plus 1 tsp dried basil	4 tbsp

In a large frying pan, bring ¼ litre (8 fl oz) of water to the boil over high heat. Add the onion, garlic and fennel seeds, and cook until the water has almost evaporated and the onions and garlic are soft — about 5 minutes. Add the oil, peppers, courgettes, saffron, the liqueur if you are using it, and 6 cl (2 fl oz) of water; continue to cook, stirring constantly, until all the vegetables are tender — about 5 minutes more. Stir in the fresh basil or the parsley and dried basil, and serve immediately.

Peeling Sweet Peppers

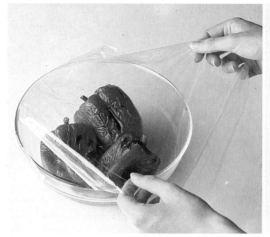

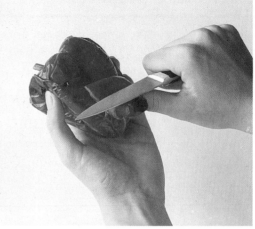

1 *LOOSENING THE SKIN. Place the peppers about 5 cm (2 inches) below a preheated grill. Turn the peppers as their sides become slightly scorched, until their skin has blistered on all sides. Transfer the peppers to a bowl and cover it with plastic film, or put them in a paper bag and fold it shut; the trapped steam will make the peppers limp and loosen their skins.*

2 *REMOVING THE SKIN. With a paring knife, peel off a pepper's skin in sections, from top to bottom. Repeat the process to skin the other peppers. The peppers may then be seeded and deribbed.*

Sweet Peppers with Herbed Rice

Serves 8
Working time: about 30 minutes
Total time: about 1 hour and 15 minutes

Calories **235**
Protein **4g**
Cholesterol **0mg**
Total fat **5g**
Saturated fat **1g**
Sodium **15mg**

6	red, yellow or green peppers, grilled and peeled (above)	6
175 g	long-grain brown rice	6 oz
1	5 cm (2 inch) strip of lemon peel	1
2 tbsp	virgin olive oil	2 tbsp
1	onion, chopped	1
90 g	raisins, soaked in 12.5 cl (4 fl oz) dry white wine	3 oz
6 cl	unsalted chicken or vegetable stock	2 fl oz
1	lemon, juice only	1
3 tbsp	chopped parsley	3 tbsp
1 tsp	fresh thyme, or ¼ tsp dried thyme	1 tsp
⅛ tsp	ground coriander	⅛ tsp

Bring 1 litre (1¾ pints) of water to the boil in a saucepan. Add the rice and the lemon peel. Simmer for 25 minutes over medium heat.

Remove the stems, ribs and seeds from the peeled peppers. Cut the peppers in half lengthwise. Set eight of the pepper halves aside as a garnish. Coarsely chop the remaining pepper halves and set them aside too. Preheat the oven to 200°C (400°F or Mark 6).

Heat 1 tablespoon of the oil in a large, heavy frying pan. Add the onion, and cook until it is translucent — about 5 minutes. Add the raisins and wine, stock, and lemon juice. Bring to the boil and add the rice. Stir in the parsley, thyme, coriander and the chopped peppers. Transfer the rice mixture to a 1.5 litre (2½ pint) gratin dish. Mound up the rice slightly and arrange the pepper halves on top. Bake the dish for 20 minutes. Brush the peppers with the remaining oil before serving.

Red and Yellow Peppers with Rocket

ROCKET, OR ARUGULA, GIVES A PUNGENT, MUSTARDY
ACCENT TO THIS DISH.

Serves 4
Working time: about 45 minutes
Total time: about 1 hour and 15 minutes

Calories **65**
Protein **3g**
Cholesterol **0mg**
Total fat **4g**
Saturated fat **1g**
Sodium **70mg**

6	sweet red and yellow peppers, grilled and peeled (left)	6
5	garlic cloves, unpeeled	5
1 tbsp	virgin olive oil	1 tbsp
1 tsp	balsamic vinegar or fresh lemon juice	1 tsp
⅛ tsp	salt	⅛ tsp
	freshly ground black pepper	
1	bunch rocket, leaves coarsely shredded (about 100 g/3 oz)	1

Preheat the oven to 180°C (350°F or Mark 4). Place the garlic cloves on a piece of aluminium foil, and sprinkle them with 1 teaspoon of the oil. Wrap them up in the foil, then bake until a clove can be pierced easily with a skewer — about 20 minutes.

Remove the stems, ribs and seeds from the peppers, working over a bowl to catch the juices. Strain the pepper juices and reserve them. Slice the peppers lengthwise into 1 cm (½ inch) wide strips.

Squeeze the softened garlic cloves out of their skins, purée them through a small strainer and add to the pepper juices. Stir in the vinegar or lemon juice, salt and pepper. Heat the remaining 2 teaspoons of oil in a large, heavy frying pan over medium-high heat. Add the rocket and cook until it wilts — about 1 minute. Add the sliced peppers and stir in the garlic mixture; cook for 1 or 2 minutes more to reheat the peppers. Transfer the peppers and rocket to a serving platter. The dish may be eaten hot, cold or at room temperature.

Chayote Squash with Tarragon

Serves 4
Working time: about 15 minutes
Total time: about 25 minutes

Calories **75**
Protein **1g**
Cholesterol **0mg**
Total fat **4g**
Saturated fat **0g**
Sodium **140mg**

500 g	chayote squash, peeled, cut in half lengthwise, large seeds removed, thinly sliced	1 lb
1 tbsp	safflower oil	1 tbsp
1	large shallot, finely chopped	1
1	garlic clove, finely chopped	1
2 tbsp	chopped fresh tarragon, or 2 tsp dried tarragon	2 tbsp
¼ tsp	salt	¼ tsp
	freshly ground black pepper	
6 cl	unsalted chicken or vegetable stock	2 fl oz

Heat the oil in a large, heavy frying pan over medium heat. Cook the shallot and garlic for 1 minute only. Add the chayote slices, tarragon, salt and pepper, and toss to mix. Pour in the stock, reduce the heat to low and simmer until the chayote is tender but still crisp — 6 to 8 minutes. Transfer the squash to a warmed vegetable dish and serve immediately.

EDITOR'S NOTE: *Small, young chayote need not be peeled.*

Spaghetti Squash with Tahini Sauce

Serves 8
Working time: about 15 minutes
Total time: about 45 minutes

Calories **75**
Protein **2g**
Cholesterol **0mg**
Total fat **5g**
Saturated fat **1g**
Sodium **20mg**

2 kg	spaghetti squash	4 lb
2 tbsp	tahini	2 tbsp
1	garlic clove, finely chopped	1
¼ tsp	Sichuan peppercorns, toasted and ground, or ⅛ tsp freshly ground black pepper	¼ tsp
⅛ tsp	cayenne pepper	⅛ tsp
1 tsp	fresh lemon juice	1 tsp
1 tbsp	safflower oil	1 tbsp
6 cl	unsalted chicken or vegetable stock	2 fl oz
1	spring onion, green part only, thinly sliced	1

Cook the spaghetti squash whole in a large saucepan of boiling water until a skewer or fork can be inserted into it easily — about 30 minutes.

While the squash is cooking, make the tahini sauce. In a small bowl, combine the tahini, garlic, Sichuan pepper or black pepper, cayenne pepper, lemon juice and safflower oil.

When the squash is done, halve it lengthwise. With a spoon, scoop out the seeds and loose fibres and discard them. Using a fork, scrape out the spaghetti-like strands of flesh and pile them on a serving platter. Bring the stock to the boil in a small saucepan, pour it into the tahini mixture, and stir to mix. Pour the sauce over the squash and toss together. Garnish with the spring onion and serve.

EDITOR'S NOTE: *Tahini, also called sesame paste, is made from roasted or unroasted ground sesame seeds. It is available in jars or cans where Middle-Eastern foods are sold.*

Yellow Squash Quiche with a Rice Crust

Serves 4 as a main dish
Working time: about 30 minutes
Total time: about 1 hour and 15 minutes

Calories **320**
Protein **17g**
Cholesterol **160mg**
Total fat **11g**
Saturated fat **5g**
Sodium **290mg**

3	yellow squashes, halved lengthwise, seeded, flesh grated	3
250 g	cooked rice	8 oz
4	eggs, whites only of 2	4
90 g	Emmenthal cheese, grated	3 oz
2 tsp	safflower oil	2 tsp
6	shallots, finely chopped	6
12.5 cl	vermouth	4 fl oz
¼ tsp	salt	¼ tsp
	freshly ground black pepper	
½ tsp	chopped fresh marjoram, or ¼ tsp dried marjoram	½ tsp
½ tsp	fresh thyme, or ¼ tsp dried thyme	½ tsp
¼ litre	skimmed milk	8 fl oz
⅛ tsp	grated nutmeg	⅛ tsp
12	thin strips of sweet red and green peppers, blanched	12

Preheat the oven to 190°C (375°F or Mark 5). To prepare the rice crust, combine the cooked rice, one of the egg whites and half of the cheese. Press the mixture into a 23 cm (9 inch) quiche or flan tin. Prebake the crust until the cheese is just melted — 3 to 4 minutes. Remove the crust from the oven and set aside.

Heat the oil in a heavy frying pan over medium heat. Cook the shallots until soft — about 2 to 3 minutes — stirring occasionally. Pour the vermouth into the pan, and cook until the vermouth has nearly evaporated — about 3 minutes. Add the squash and cook, stirring occasionally, until the squash is tender — about 3 minutes. Season the mixture with the salt, pepper, marjoram and thyme, and remove from the heat.

In a large mixing bowl, lightly beat the two whole eggs, the remaining egg white, the skimmed milk and nutmeg. Stir in the remaining cheese and the squash mixture. Pour this mixture into the crust and bake until the filling begins to set — about 20 minutes. Remove the quiche from the oven and arrange the pepper strips on top. Return the quiche to the oven and bake until the filling is set in the centre — 5 to 7 minutes more. Cut the quiche into wedges and serve.

Pumpkin Purée
with Orange and Ginger

Serves 6
Working time: about 30 minutes
Total time: about 1 hour and 30 minutes

Calories **110**
Protein **2g**
Cholesterol **10mg**
Total fat **4g**
Saturated fat **2g**
Sodium **90mg**

1.75 kg	pumpkin, or butternut squash, peeled, seeded and cut into 1 cm (½ inch) cubes	3½ lb
1½ tbsp	unsalted butter	1½ tbsp
¼ tsp	salt	¼ tsp
¼ litre	fresh orange juice with pulp	8 fl oz
1 tbsp	fresh lime juice	1 tbsp
1½ tbsp	finely chopped fresh ginger root	1½ tbsp

Melt the butter in a heavy frying pan over medium heat. Add the pumpkin and sprinkle with the salt. Cook for 20 minutes, stirring often. Add the juices and ginger. Continue cooking, stirring frequently, until the mixture has reached a dense, pasty consistency — about 35 minutes. Purée the mixture in a food processor or blender, or through a sieve or food mill. Transfer to a piping bag fitted with a large star nozzle and pipe it into a vegetable dish. Or spoon the purée into the dish and decorate the surface with the back of a spoon.

Yellow Squash with
Peppered Dill Sauce

Serves 6
Working time: about 40 minutes
Total time: about 45 minutes

Calories **55**
Protein **2g**
Cholesterol **10mg**
Total fat **3g**
Saturated fat **2g**
Sodium **20mg**

750 g	medium yellow squash or courgettes, halved lengthwise, seeded and cut into 1 cm (½ inch) pieces	1½ lb
25 g	unsalted butter	¾ oz
1½ tbsp	flour	1½ tbsp
¼ litre	unsalted chicken or vegetable stock	8 fl oz
45 g	fresh dill, coarsely chopped, plus 2 tbsp finely chopped fresh dill	1½ oz
2 tsp	fresh lemon juice	2 tsp
¼ tsp	cayenne pepper	¼ tsp
	white pepper	

Pour enough water into a saucepan to fill it about 2.5 cm (1 inch) deep. Set a vegetable steamer in the pan and bring the water to the boil. Put the squash in the steamer, cover the pan, and steam the squash until just tender — about 4 minutes. Remove the steamer and squash; pour out any water remaining in the pan. Return the squash to the pan and cover to keep it warm.

To prepare the sauce, melt the butter over medium heat in a small, heavy-bottomed saucepan. Add the flour and whisk until the mixture bubbles — about 1 minute. Stir in the stock and bring it to the boil, stirring constantly. Add the coarsely chopped dill and cook for 3

minutes more. Stir in 1 teaspoon of the lemon juice along with the cayenne pepper and white pepper. Strain the sauce over the squash in the pan, then stir in the remaining lemon juice and the finely chopped dill. Add more white pepper and serve immediately.

Breaded Courgette Slices with Cheese

Serves 12 as an hors d'oeuvre
Working time: about 30 minutes
Total time: about 40 minutes

Calories **45**
Protein **3g**
Cholesterol **5mg**
Total fat **3g**
Saturated fat **0g**
Sodium **80mg**

500 g	courgettes, cut on the diagonal into 5 mm (¼ inch) slices	1 lb
	freshly ground black pepper	
60 g	pecorino or Parmesan cheese, freshly grated	2 oz
30 g	fresh breadcrumbs	1 oz
1 tbsp	chopped fresh oregano, or 1 tsp dried oregano	1 tbsp
3	egg whites, beaten until frothy	3
2 tbsp	safflower oil	2 tbsp

Preheat the oven to 160°C (325°F or Mark 3). Grind pepper liberally over the courgette slices. In a shallow bowl, combine the cheese, breadcrumbs and oregano. Dip half the slices into the beaten egg whites, then coat them evenly with the cheese-crumb mixture and set aside.

Heat 1 tablespoon of the oil in a large, shallow fireproof casserole over medium-high heat. Use a pastry brush to distribute the oil evenly over the bottom. Place the breaded slices in the casserole and put it immediately into the oven. After 5 minutes, carefully turn the slices over and bake them until they are golden-brown — 5 to 7 minutes more. Remove to a warmed platter and repeat with the remaining courgettes. Serve hot.

Courgettes Sautéed with Shallots and Tomato Strips

Serves 6
Working (and total) time: about 35 minutes

Calories **75**
Protein **2g**
Cholesterol **0mg**
Total fat **5g**
Saturated fat **1g**
Sodium **95mg**

600 g	courgettes, ends trimmed	1¼ lb
1	large ripe tomato, skinned (page 84)	1
2 tbsp	virgin olive oil	2 tbsp
¼ tsp	salt	¼ tsp
	freshly ground black pepper	
6	shallots, thinly sliced	6
2 tbsp	chopped parsley or fresh coriander	2 tbsp
1 tbsp	fresh lemon juice	1 tbsp

Put the skinned tomato stem end down on a cutting board. With a small, sharp knife, cut wide strips of flesh from the tomato, discarding the seeds and core. Slice the flesh into 5 mm (¼ inch) wide strips and set them aside.

Slice the courgettes into 5 cm (2 inch) rounds. Cut each round into six wedges.

Heat the oil in a large, heavy frying pan over medium-high heat. When the oil is hot, add the courgettes. Cook, stirring frequently, for 5 minutes. Sprinkle the courgettes with the salt and pepper; add the shallots and cook for another 3 minutes, stirring often. Add the tomato strips, the parsley or coriander, and the lemon juice. Cook for 4 minutes more to blend the flavours, and serve immediately.

Baked Courgettes with Coriander Pesto

Serves 6
Working time: about 15 minutes
Total time: about 40 minutes

Calories **65**
Protein **3g**
Cholesterol **5mg**
Total fat **4g**
Saturated fat **1g**
Sodium **155mg**

6	small courgettes (about 750 g/1½ lb)	6
25 g	fresh coriander, chopped	¾ oz
25 g	parsley, chopped	¾ oz
1 tbsp	pine-nuts	1 tbsp
1	garlic clove	1
¼ tsp	salt	¼ tsp
	freshly ground black pepper	
1 tbsp	virgin olive oil	1 tbsp
30 g	Parmesan cheese, freshly grated	1 oz

Preheat the oven to 160°C (325°F or Mark 3).

To make the pesto, combine the coriander, parsley, pine-nuts, garlic, salt and pepper in a food processor or blender. Purée until smooth — about 3 minutes. Add the oil and blend for 1 minute. Add the Parmesan and blend 2 minutes more.

Trim the courgettes and cut them in half lengthwise. Spread the pesto on the exposed flesh of one half of each courgette, and cover with the other half. Wrap the courgettes in aluminium foil. Bake them until just tender — 20 to 25 minutes.

Spring Vegetable Stir-Fry

Serves 4
Working time: about 30 minutes
Total time: about 30 minutes

Calories **170**
Protein **7g**
Cholesterol **0mg**
Total fat **8g**
Saturated fat **1g**
Sodium **170mg**

2 tbsp	virgin olive oil	2 tbsp
30 g	pine-nuts (optional)	1 oz
30 g	fresh ginger root, peeled and finely chopped	1 oz
2	garlic cloves, crushed	2
125 g	French beans, topped and tailed	4 oz
125 g	mange-tout, topped and tailed	4 oz
125 g	broccoli florets (optional)	4 oz
125 g	asparagus, trimmed, stems finely sliced diagonally	4 oz
125 g	carrots, peeled, thinly sliced diagonally	4 oz
½ each	small sweet red, green and yellow peppers, seeded and finely sliced	½ each
3	sticks celery, thinly sliced	3
3	spring onions, trimmed, thinly sliced diagonally	3
¼ tsp	salt	¼ tsp

Heat 1 teaspoon of the oil in a large frying pan. Add the pine-nuts and fry gently until they turn golden-brown. Remove them from the pan and set them aside.

Pour 1 tablespoon of oil into the pan and heat. Add the ginger and garlic and cook for 2 to 3 seconds, then add the beans and stir-fry for about 2 minutes. Add the mange-tout, stir-fry for 1 minute, then add the broccoli, asparagus and carrots, and stir-fry for 2 minutes more. Add the remaining oil, the peppers, celery, and spring onions, and stir-fry until the vegetables are just tender — 2 to 3 minutes. Season with the salt, and stir in the reserved pine-nuts.

Transfer to a hot serving dish and garnish, if liked, with finely sliced spring onions. Serve immediately.

Summer Vegetable Stew

Serves 10
Working time: about 40 minutes
Total time: about 1 hour

Calories **115**
Protein **4g**
Cholesterol **5mg**
Total fat **6g**
Saturated fat **1g**
Sodium **145mg**

3 tbsp	safflower oil	3 tbsp
8	small shallots, peeled	8
250 g	mushrooms, wiped clean, left whole if small, halved or quartered if large	8 oz
1	yellow squash or courgette, cut into 2.5 cm (1 inch) cubes	1
2	sticks celery, cut into 2.5 cm (1 inch) pieces	2
1	sweet red pepper, seeded, deribbed and cut into 2.5 cm (1 inch) wide strips	1
1	small aubergine, cut into 2.5 cm (1 inch) cubes	1
2	garlic cloves, finely chopped	2
2	medium tomatoes, skinned, seeded (page 84) and chopped	2
12.5 cl	dry vermouth	4 fl oz
½ tsp	salt	½ tsp
	freshly ground black pepper	
1	small potato, peeled and grated	1
1	ear of sweetcorn, cut into 2.5 cm (1 inch) pieces	1
250 g	young carrots, peeled	8 oz
250 g	French beans, topped and tailed	8 oz
1	bay leaf	1
⅛ tsp	saffron threads, steeped in 6 cl (2 fl oz) hot water	⅛ tsp
2 tbsp	chopped fresh marjoram, or 2 tsp dried marjoram	2 tbsp
60 g	Parmesan cheese, freshly grated	2 oz

Heat 1 tablespoon of the oil in a large, heavy frying pan or shallow fireproof casserole over high heat. Sauté the shallots in the oil until they are lightly coloured — about 1 minute. Add the mushrooms, squash, celery and red pepper, and sauté for 2 minutes, stirring frequently. Transfer to a bowl and set aside.

Heat the remaining oil in the pan over high heat; add the aubergine and sauté it for 2 minutes. Stir in the garlic and cook it very briefly — no more than 15 seconds. Return the vegetables in the bowl to the pan and stir in the tomatoes and vermouth. Cook the liquid until it is slightly reduced — about 5 minutes. Add the salt and pepper.

Stir the potato into the vegetables together with the sweetcorn, carrots, beans, bay leaf and just enough water to cover them. Simmer, uncovered, until the vegetables are tender — 25 to 30 minutes. Stir in the saffron mixture and the marjoram. Just before serving, sprinkle the stew with the Parmesan cheese.

Charcoal-Grilled Vegetables with Herb Marinade

Serves 12
Working (and total) time: about 45 minutes

Calories **90**
Protein **3g**
Cholesterol **0mg**
Total fat **5g**
Saturated fat **1g**
Sodium **50mg**

6	medium, or 12 small, courgettes	6
3	medium onions	3
12	large mushroom caps	12
4	sweet red peppers	4
6	ripe plum tomatoes, halved	6
3	limes, each cut into 8 wedges	3

Herb marinade		
6 cl	virgin olive oil	2 fl oz
1 tbsp	fresh rosemary, or 1 tsp dried rosemary	1 tbsp
1 tsp	fresh thyme, or ½ tsp dried thyme	1 tsp
¼ tsp	crushed hot red pepper flakes	¼ tsp
¼ tsp	salt	¼ tsp

About 30 minutes before you plan to cook the vegetables, prepare the charcoal for grilling.

To make the herb marinade, put the oil, rosemary, thyme, red pepper flakes and salt in a small saucepan. Warm the mixture over medium heat until it begins to

bubble gently, then cook it for 4 minutes more. Remove the marinade from the heat and let it stand while you prepare the vegetables.

If medium-sized, slice the courgettes in half crosswise with a diagonal cut through the middle. Cut each half or whole courgette into a fan by making lengthwise slices 5 mm (¼ inch) apart, leaving the slices attached at the uncut end.

Cut the onions lengthwise into quarters. Thread the onions on to one or two skewers. Wipe the mushroom caps clean and thread them on to a skewer. Cut the sweet red peppers lengthwise into thirds, then derib and seed them. Thread the peppers on to one or two

skewers. Thread the tomato halves on to a skewer.

When the charcoal grill is hot, lightly brush all the vegetables with the marinade. Cook the vegetables, staggering their cooking times so that they will all be ready at once. Put the courgette fans on the grill first — they require about 10 minutes' grilling. After 2 minutes, add the onions; after another 2 minutes, add the mushrooms. Add the peppers and tomatoes for the last 4 minutes' grilling. Baste the vegetables with marinade as they cook, and turn them as they brown.

Remove the vegetables from their skewers and arrange them on a platter. Serve them hot, accompanied by the lime wedges.

Vegetable Mosaic

Serves 10
Working time: about 45 minutes
Total time: about 2 hours

Calories **120**
Protein **4g**
Cholesterol **0mg**
Total fat **6g**
Saturated fat **1g**
Sodium **195mg**

850 g	large onions, thinly sliced	1¾ lb
2	fennel bulbs, green stems removed and feathery green tops reserved, bulbs halved lengthwise and thinly sliced	2
¾ tsp	salt	¾ tsp
	freshly ground black pepper	
1 tbsp	fresh rosemary, or ¾ tsp dried rosemary, crumbled	1 tbsp
6 cl	cider vinegar	2 fl oz
600 g	courgettes, cut diagonally into 5 mm (¼ inch) thick slices	1¼ lb
2	garlic cloves, finely chopped	2
2 tbsp	chopped fresh oregano, or 2 tsp dried oregano	2 tbsp
6	ripe plum tomatoes	6
600 g	small aubergines, halved lengthwise, cut into 1 cm (½ inch) thick slices	1¼ lb
4 tbsp	virgin olive oil	4 tbsp

Put the onions and bulb fennel in a large, heavy-bottomed fireproof casserole with ¼ teaspoon of the salt, some pepper and half of the rosemary. Pour in the vinegar and 6 cl (2 fl oz) of water. Cook the vegetables over medium heat, scraping the bottom of the pan frequently to mix in any caramelized bits, until the vegetables are well browned — 30 to 35 minutes.

Meanwhile, prepare the other vegetables. Preheat the grill. Toss the courgette slices in a bowl with the garlic, half the oregano and ¼ teaspoon of the salt. Cut the tomatoes into slices 5 mm (¼ inch) thick. Put the slices on a plate and sprinkle them with some pepper and the remaining salt. Put the aubergine slices on a baking sheet and brush them with 1 tablespoon of the oil. Grill them 5 to 7.5 cm (2 to 3 inches) from the heat source until they are very brown — about 8 minutes. Turn the aubergine slices and brush them with another tablespoon of the oil. Grill the aubergine slices on the second side until they are brown — 6 to 7 minutes. Preheat the oven to 190°C (375°F or Mark 5).

Spread the browned onions and fennel in the bottom of a large, shallow baking dish. Arrange the aubergine, courgette and tomato slices on top of the onions. Dribble 1 tablespoon of the oil over the vegetables and cover the dish with aluminium foil, shiny side down.

Bake the vegetables for 25 minutes. Remove the foil and dribble the remaining oil over the top. Continue to bake the vegetables, uncovered, until they are soft — about 20 minutes. Sprinkle the vegetables with the remaining rosemary and oregano, and bake them for 10 minutes more. Garnish the finished dish with the reserved fennel tops.

(or 2 teaspoons of dried basil), salt and pepper. Stirring occasionally, cook the mixture until the celery is limp — about 4 minutes. Stir in the tomatoes and cook them, stirring occasionally, until they have softened — about 5 minutes. Add the brown sugar and the bread cubes, and combine. Place the mixture in a shallow baking dish and bake until the top is nicely dry — 35 to 40 minutes. Serve garnished with the remaining fresh basil, if you are using it, or sprinkle the dish with the chopped parsley.

Stewed Tomatoes with Cubed Rye Bread

Serves 6
Working time: about 20 minutes
Total time: about 1 hour

Calories **115**
Protein **3g**
Cholesterol **0mg**
Total fat **3g**
Saturated fat **0g**
Sodium **170mg**

6	tomatoes, skinned, seeded (right) and coarsely chopped	6
1 tbsp	virgin olive oil	1 tbsp
1	onion, finely chopped	1
2	sticks celery, finely chopped	2
2	garlic cloves, finely chopped	2
2 tbsp	chopped fresh basil, or 2 tsp dried basil plus 1½ tsp chopped parsley	2 tbsp
¼ tsp	salt	¼ tsp
	freshly ground black pepper	
2 tbsp	dark brown sugar	2 tbsp
30 g	dark rye bread, cubed	1 oz

Preheat the oven to 180°C (350°F or Mark 4). In a large, heavy frying pan, heat the oil over medium-low heat. Add the onion, celery, garlic, 1½ tablespoons of the basil

Peeling and Seeding a Tomato

1 *SKINNING THE TOMATO. Core the tomato by cutting a conical plug from its stem end. Cut a shallow cross in the base. Immerse the tomato in boiling water for 10 to 30 seconds, then plunge it into cold water. When the tomato has cooled, peel the skin away from the cross in sections.*

2 *SEEDING THE TOMATO. Halve the skinned tomato. Gently squeeze one of the halves, forcing out its seeds and juice. Rotate the tomato 90 degrees and squeeze once more. Dislodge any seeds from the inner chambers. Repeat the process with the other half.*

Baked Tomatoes with Herbed Mushrooms

Serves 4
Working time: about 45 minutes
Total time: about 1 hour

Calories **125**
Protein **6g**
Cholesterol **5mg**
Total fat **6g**
Saturated fat **1g**
Sodium **205mg**

4	ripe, firm, unblemished medium tomatoes	4
5 tsp	finely chopped fresh basil, or 1½ tsp dried basil	5 tsp
4 tsp	virgin olive oil	4 tsp
300 g	mushrooms, wiped clean, trimmed and very finely chopped	10 oz
2	shallots, very finely chopped	2
2	garlic cloves, very finely chopped	2
1 tbsp	chopped fresh oregano, or 1 tsp dried oregano	1 tbsp
	freshly ground black pepper	
¼ litre	unsalted chicken or vegetable stock	8 fl oz
1½ tbsp	freshly grated Parmesan cheese	1½ tbsp
¼ tsp	salt	¼ tsp

Cut a 2 cm (¾ inch) slice from the stem end of each tomato and set the slices aside. To make room for the stuffing, cut some of the flesh from the centre of each tomato. Chop the flesh and place it in a small bowl with 2 teaspoons of the fresh basil or ½ teaspoon of the dried basil. Set the bowl aside. Remove the remaining seeds from the tomatoes.

Preheat the oven to 180°C (350°F or Mark 4). In a heavy frying pan, heat 3 teaspoons of the oil over medium heat. Add the mushrooms, shallots, garlic, the remaining basil, the oregano and the pepper. Reduce the heat to medium low, cover the pan, and cook for 2 minutes. Then uncover the pan and cook the mixture further, stirring occasionally, until all the moisture has evaporated — about 8 minutes more.

Meanwhile, pour the stock into a saucepan and bring it to the boil. Reduce the liquid to 6 cl (2 fl oz). Add the tomato-basil mixture and cook until the mixture is reduced to a thick purée — 3 to 4 minutes. Strain the purée through a fine-mesh sieve into the mushroom mixture and stir in 1 tablespoon of the grated Parmesan cheese.

Sprinkle the insides of the tomatoes with the salt and stuff them with the mushroom-tomato mixture. Replace the tomato tops and set the tomatoes in a baking dish. Brush them with the remaining oil, and bake until tender — 15 to 20 minutes. Serve hot, with the remaining cheese sprinkled over the stuffing and the tomato tops put back on.

4 Stuffed with spinach, pine-nuts and currants, six plump onions suggest just how delicious bulbs, roots and tubers can be when prepared with flair.

Down-to-Earth Delights

Their botanical designation as roots, tubers and bulbs does little to glamorize them, but the earthy vegetables that fall within this broad category count as some of the most enjoyed and used of all vegetables. Try to imagine getting along without just two of them: the carrot and the potato. Not only are these staples that can be cooked and eaten in a variety of ways, they are storehouses of nutrition.

Only 100 g (3 oz) of raw carrot provides two and a half times the Recommended Daily Amount of vitamin A — in the form of carotene, which the body converts to the vitamin.

The potato is even more nutritious. It contains major amounts of vitamins B_6 and C, phosphorus, iron and magnesium, as well as potassium, zinc, copper and iodine. The potato is also an important source of complex carbohydrates. Long maligned as being fattening, it has in fact relatively few calories; a medium-sized baked potato, for example, has about 110 calories — no more than a large apple.

A still more nutritious tuber is the neglected yellow or deep orange sweet potato. One of nature's most complete foods, the sweet potato provides double the RDA of vitamin A, almost all the RDA of vitamin C, and it also contains vitamin B_6, iron, potassium and fibre.

If both the sweet and the white potato are good for you, those two familiar bulbs, garlic and onions, may be the next best thing to medicine — or so say their most ardent fans. Some studies have suggested that in addition to possessing anti-bacterial properties, garlic may lower blood cholesterol levels and reduce the likelihood of blood clots. Onions are thought to have similarly beneficial effects, but experiments have yet to be carried out proving the medicinal value of either. Suffice it to say that, when cooked, onions can be as sweet and subtle as their close relative, the leek.

The leek is only one of the many vegetables in the root, tuber and bulb category deserving greater use in the kitchen. Among others are salsify and scorzonera, long roots with an oyster-like taste; the knobbly celeriac, or celery root; the sweet parsnip; the crunchy Jerusalem artichoke; and the crisp water chestnut. They and others — including three old stand-bys: the beetroot, turnip and swede — are at the core of the 33 recipes that fill this chapter with delectable surprises.

Aromatic Potatoes and Leeks

Serves 6
Working time: about 30 minutes
Total time: about 2 hours

Calories **205**
Protein **5g**
Cholesterol **5mg**
Total fat **1g**
Saturated fat **0g**
Sodium **125mg**

1.5 kg	potatoes, peeled and sliced into 5 mm (¼ inch) rounds	3 lb
½ litre	unsalted chicken or vegetable stock	16 fl oz
3	leeks, trimmed, cleaned (page 110) and cut into 5 mm (¼ inch) pieces	3
3	garlic cloves, finely chopped	3
1½ tsp	fresh rosemary, or ½ tsp dried rosemary	1½ tsp
½ tsp	chopped fresh savory, or ¼ tsp dried savory	½ tsp
1 tsp	fresh thyme, or ¼ tsp dried thyme	1 tsp
¼ tsp	salt	¼ tsp
	freshly ground black pepper	
1	lemon, juice only	1

Preheat the oven to 220°C (425°F or Mark 7). In a small saucepan, combine the stock, leeks and garlic; bring the liquid to the boil, lower the heat and simmer for 3 minutes. Strain, reserving both liquid and solids.

Combine the rosemary, savory, thyme, salt and pepper in a small bowl. Arrange one third of the potatoes in a layer in a baking dish. Spread half the leek mixture over the potatoes, then sprinkle with half the herb mixture. Arrange half the remaining potatoes in a second layer and top with the remaining leek and herb mixture. Add the rest of the potatoes in a final layer. Pour the lemon juice and the reserved stock over all.

Cover the dish with foil and bake it for 30 minutes. Uncover the dish and return it to the oven until the top turns crisp and golden — about 1 hour more.

Oven-Baked French Fries

THIS RECIPE USES A MERE 2 TEASPOONS OF OIL TO PRODUCE A SATISFYING ALTERNATIVE TO FAT-LADEN POTATO CHIPS.

Serves 4
Working time: about 15 minutes
Total time: about 1 hour

Calories **105**
Protein **2g**
Cholesterol **0mg**
Total fat **3g**
Saturated fat **0g**
Sodium **145mg**

750 g	large potatoes, scrubbed	1½ lb
1 tsp	chili powder	1 tsp
2 tsp	safflower oil	2 tsp
¼ tsp	salt	¼ tsp

Put a large baking sheet in the oven and preheat the oven to 240°C (475°F or Mark 9). Cut the potatoes lengthwise into slices about 1 cm (½ inch) thick. Cut each slice lengthwise into 1 cm (½ inch) strips and put them in a large bowl. Toss the strips with the chili powder to coat them evenly; sprinkle on the oil and toss again.

Arrange the potato strips in a single layer on the hot baking sheet. Bake the strips for 20 minutes, then turn them and continue baking until they are crisp and browned — about 20 minutes more. Sprinkle the French fries with the salt and serve them hot.

Potato Swirls

Serves 8
Working time: about 20 minutes
Total time: about 1 hour and 30 minutes

Calories **75**
Protein **3g**
Cholesterol **5mg**
Total fat **2g**
Saturated fat **0g**
Sodium **90mg**

850 g	potatoes, scrubbed	1¾ lb
1	garlic clove, finely chopped	1
1 tbsp	virgin olive oil	1 tbsp
2	egg whites, lightly beaten	2
¼ tsp	grated nutmeg	¼ tsp
¼ tsp	salt	¼ tsp
¼ tsp	white pepper	¼ tsp
12.5 cl	plain low-fat yogurt	4 fl oz
2 tbsp	finely cut chives	2 tbsp

Preheat the oven to 200°C (400°F or Mark 6). Prick the potatoes and bake them until they are tender — about 1 hour. When the potatoes are cool enough to handle, scoop out the flesh and work it through a food mill or a sieve to achieve a smooth purée. (Puréeing the potatoes in a food processor or blender would make them gluey.)

Combine the garlic and oil in a small saucepan over medium heat and cook for 1 or 2 minutes (this softens the garlic and mellows its flavour). Add the garlic and oil to the potatoes with the egg whites, nutmeg, salt and pepper. Transfer the mixture to a piping bag fitted with a large star nozzle. Pipe eight rounds about 5 cm (2 inches) in diameter on to an oiled baking sheet. Pipe a raised border on the edge of each round. (If you do not have a piping bag, form the potato mixture into eight mounds and make an indentation in the top of each with the back of a spoon.)

Bake the potato swirls until the edges are crisp and brown — 7 to 10 minutes. With a spatula, transfer the swirls to a serving platter or individual plates. Combine the yogurt and the cut chives in a small bowl, and spoon this mixture into the centre of each swirl. Serve the potato swirls hot.

Baked Potatoes Hungarian-Style

Serves 4
Working time: about 15 minutes
Total time: about 1 hour and 15 minutes

Calories **130**
Protein **5g**
Cholesterol **2mg**
Total fat **1g**
Saturated fat **0g**
Sodium **170mg**

4	medium potatoes, scrubbed	4
12.5 cl	unsalted chicken or vegetable stock	4 fl oz
1	onion, finely chopped	1
2	garlic cloves, finely chopped	2
1½ tsp	paprika	1½ tsp
12.5 cl	plain low-fat yogurt	4 fl oz
¼ tsp	salt	¼ tsp
	freshly ground black pepper	

Preheat the oven to 200°C (400°F or Mark 6). Prick the potatoes and bake them for 1 hour.

Near the end of the baking time, combine the stock, onion and garlic in a saucepan. Bring to the boil and cook until the onions are tender — about 5 minutes.

When the potatoes are done, cut a lengthwise slice off the top of each one. Hollow out each potato, forming shells about 5 mm (¼ inch) thick.

To prepare the stuffing, stir the scooped-out potato flesh into the onion mixture in the saucepan. Add 1¼ teaspoons of the paprika, 6 cl (2 fl oz) of the yogurt, the salt and pepper, and stir well. Work the mixture through a food mill or a sieve to achieve a smooth stuffing.

Loosely fill the potato shells with the stuffing and reheat them in the oven for 10 minutes. Just before serving the stuffed potatoes, top them with the remaining yogurt and sprinkle them with the remaining ¼ teaspoon of paprika.

Water Chestnut Fritters

Serves 6 as an appetizer (about 5 fritters per serving)
Working time: about 30 minutes
Total time: about 45 minutes

Calories **125**
Protein **5g**
Cholesterol **10mg**
Total fat **6g**
Saturated fat **1g**
Sodium **128mg**

500 g	fresh water chestnuts	1 lb
1 tsp	sugar, dissolved in 1 litre (1¾ pints) cold water	1 tsp
90 g	uncooked chicken breast meat, coarsely chopped	3 oz
125 g	mushrooms, stemmed	4 oz
1	spring onion, trimmed and chopped	1
2 tbsp	finely chopped fresh ginger root	2 tbsp
1	garlic clove, finely chopped	1
1 tbsp	low-sodium soy sauce, or naturally fermented shoyu	1 tbsp
2 tbsp	peanut oil	2 tbsp
Ginger-garlic dip		
1 tbsp	finely chopped fresh ginger root	1 tbsp
1	garlic clove, finely chopped	1
12.5 cl	rice vinegar	4 fl oz
½ tsp	dark sesame oil	½ tsp
6	thin carrot rounds	6

Peel the water chestnuts with a small, sharp knife, and drop them into the sugared water as you work. (The sugar in the water will help preserve the water chestnuts' natural sweetness.)

Preheat the oven to 180°C (350°F or Mark 4). Put the chicken, mushrooms, spring onion, ginger, garlic and soy sauce in a food processor or blender. Purée the mixture, stopping occasionally to scrape down the sides, until it is smooth — about 4 minutes. Transfer the purée to a mixing bowl. Chop the chestnuts coarsely and combine them with the purée. With your hands, mould the mixture into balls about 2.5 cm (1 inch) in diameter (there will be 25 to 30 of these).

Heat the peanut oil in a large, shallow fireproof casserole over medium-high heat. Brown the fritters on one side for about 2 minutes. Turn them over and put the casserole in the oven. Bake the fritters until they are browned and cooked through — 5 to 7 minutes.

Meanwhile, make the dipping sauce. Whisk together the ginger, garlic, vinegar and sesame oil in a small bowl. Float the carrot rounds on top.

Arrange the fritters on a platter and serve them with the ginger-garlic dip.

EDITOR'S NOTE: Although canned water chestnuts may be used, fresh ones are sweeter and have more flavour.

Transfer the contents of the pan to a food processor or blender. Purée the mixture, stopping two or three times to scrape down the sides. Transfer the purée to a bowl and stir in the egg yolk.

In a separate metal bowl, beat the egg whites until soft peaks form. Fold the beaten whites into the purée and pour the mixture into a lightly buttered 2 litre (3½ pint) gratin dish. Bake the mousse for 30 minutes. Serve the mousse immediately.

Sweet Potato and Pear Mousse

Serves 8
Working time: about 30 minutes
Total time: about 1 hour and 45 minutes

Calories **195**
Protein **3g**
Cholesterol **40mg**
Total fat **3g**
Saturated fat **1g**
Sodium **25mg**

1 kg	sweet potatoes	2 lb
2	large ripe pears, peeled, cored and cut into 2.5 cm (1 inch) cubes	2
3 tbsp	fresh lemon juice	3 tbsp
½ tsp	curry powder	½ tsp
½ tsp	cinnamon	½ tsp
15 g	unsalted butter	½ oz
275 g	chopped onion	9 oz
¼ litre	apple juice	8 fl oz
	freshly ground black pepper	
1	egg yolk	1
2	egg whites	2

Preheat the oven to 230°C (450°F or Mark 8). Prick the sweet potatoes and bake them until they have begun to soften — about 30 minutes. Remove the sweet potatoes from the oven and set them aside to cool. Reduce the oven temperature to 180°C (350°F or Mark 4).

In a large bowl, combine the pears, lemon juice, curry powder and cinnamon. When the sweet potatoes are cool enough to handle, cut them in half lengthwise. Peel the sweet potatoes, cut them into 2.5 cm (1 inch) cubes and add them to the bowl.

Heat the butter in a large, heavy frying pan over medium heat. Add the onion and cook it for 5 minutes, then stir in the apple juice, the sweet potato mixture and freshly ground black pepper. Cover the pan, leaving the lid slightly ajar, and cook the mixture for 15 minutes, stirring occasionally.

Spicy Sweet Potatoes and Peas

Serves 6
Working (and total) time: about 30 minutes

Calories **130**
Protein **2g**
Cholesterol **5mg**
Total fat **6g**
Saturated fat **2g**
Sodium **100mg**

600 g	sweet potatoes, peeled and cut into 1 cm (½ inch) cubes	1¼ lb
2 tsp	honey	2 tsp
3 tbsp	cider vinegar	3 tbsp
¾ tsp	chili powder	¾ tsp
½ tsp	cinnamon	½ tsp
1½ tbsp	safflower oil	1½ tbsp
175 g	onion, chopped	6 oz
15 g	unsalted butter	½ oz
¼ tsp	salt	¼ tsp
125 g	shelled fresh or frozen peas	4 oz

In a small bowl, mix together the honey, 2 tablespoons of the vinegar, the chili powder and cinnamon. Set the honey mixture aside.

Heat the oil in a large, heavy frying pan over medium-low heat. Add the sweet potatoes and cook, stirring occasionally, for 5 minutes. Raise the heat to medium high and cook for another 5 minutes, stirring frequently to prevent the sweet potatoes from sticking. Add the onion, butter, salt, the remaining vinegar and 6 cl (2 fl oz) of water. If you are using fresh peas, add them at this point. Cook, stirring constantly, until the onion just begins to brown — about 5 minutes.

Pour the honey mixture over the vegetables; if you are using frozen peas, stir them in now. Cook the vegetables, stirring constantly, for another 2 minutes and then transfer them to a serving dish.

Scorzonera with Mixed Herbs

Serves 6
Working time: about 30 minutes
Total time: about 45 minutes

Calories **100**
Protein **3g**
Cholesterol **5mg**
Total fat **2g**
Saturated fat **1g**
Sodium **190mg**

750 g	scorzonera, scrubbed well	1½ lb
1	lemon, juice only	1
30 g	flour	1 oz
½ tsp	salt	½ tsp
15 g	unsalted butter	½ oz
⅛ tsp	white pepper	⅛ tsp
1 tsp	chopped fresh thyme, or ¼ tsp dried thyme	1 tsp
1 tsp	chopped fresh marjoram, or ¼ tsp dried marjoram	1 tsp
1 tsp	finely cut chives	1 tsp
1 tsp	chopped parsley	1 tsp

To keep the scorzonera from discolouring, add the lemon juice to 2 litres (3½ pints) of very cold water.

Peel the scorzonera with a vegetable peeler and cut them in half, dropping the pieces into the acidulated water as you work.

To cook the scorzonera, first prepare a *blanc* — a cooking liquid that keeps the vegetable from discolouring. Put the flour in a large non-reactive saucepan and stir in just enough of the acidulated water to make a paste; then stir in the rest of the water. Add the scorzonera and half the salt. Bring to the boil, stirring occasionally to keep the flour from forming lumps. Cook until tender — 10 to 12 minutes — and drain.

Melt the butter in a large, heavy frying pan over high heat. Add the scorzonera, and shake the pan back and forth over the heat to coat it with the butter — about 1 minute. Then season with the remaining salt, the pepper and the herbs. Cook for 30 seconds longer to release the herbs' bouquet. Serve immediately.

EDITOR'S NOTE: *Scorzonera is similar to the lighter-skinned salsify, which can be used instead in this recipe.*

Honey-Glazed Shallots with Mint

Serves 4
Working time: about 15 minutes
Total time: about 45 minutes

Calories **150**
Protein **5g**
Cholesterol **10mg**
Total fat **3g**
Saturated fat **2g**
Sodium **165mg**

600 g	shallots, tips and root ends cut off, papery skin and all outer membranes removed to expose the cloves	1 ¼ lb
15 g	unsalted butter	½ oz
1 tbsp	honey	1 tbsp
¼ tsp	salt	¼ tsp
	freshly ground black pepper	
¼ litre	unsalted chicken or vegetable stock	8 fl oz
1 tbsp	chopped fresh mint, or 1 tsp dried mint	1 tbsp

In a heavy frying pan large enough to hold the shallots in a single layer, melt the butter over medium heat. Stir in the honey and add the shallots, salt and pepper. Pour in the stock and bring the liquid to a simmer. Cook until almost all the liquid has evaporated — about 30 minutes. Stir in the mint and serve.

Marbled Carrot and Courgette Soufflé

Serves 12 as a side dish, 6 as a main dish
Working time: about 45 minutes
Total time: about 1 hour and 30 minutes

Calories **90**
Protein **6g**
Cholesterol **30mg**
Total fat **4g**
Saturated fat **2g**
Sodium **170mg**

1 kg	carrots, peeled and sliced into 5 mm (¼ inch) rounds	2 lb
2	medium onions, coarsely chopped, plus 45 g (1½ oz) finely chopped onion	2
15 g	unsalted butter	½ oz
750 g	courgettes, seeded and grated	1½ lb
	freshly ground black pepper	
12.5 cl	semi-skimmed milk	4 fl oz
125 g	Parmesan or Romano cheese, freshly grated	4 oz
1 tsp	sugar	1 tsp
1	egg yolk	1
5	egg whites	5

Butter a 2 litre (3½ pint) soufflé dish and flour it lightly. Put the dish in the refrigerator.

Pour enough water into a saucepan to fill it about 2.5 cm (1 inch) deep. Set a vegetable steamer in the pan and bring the water to the boil. Put the carrots in the steamer, with the coarsely chopped onions on top of them. Steam the vegetables until the carrots are very soft — about 20 minutes.

While the carrots are steaming, melt the butter in a large, heavy frying pan over high heat. Add the finely chopped onion, then the courgettes and some pepper.

Cook the mixture, stirring frequently, until all of the liquid has evaporated — 5 to 7 minutes. Transfer the mixture to a bowl. Stir in 6 cl (2 fl oz) of the milk and 45 g (1½ oz) of the cheese. Set the bowl aside.

Transfer the carrots and onions to a food processor and process them for 30 seconds, stopping after 15 seconds to scrape down the sides. Pour in the remaining milk and the sugar, and purée the mixture for 1 minute more. Transfer the mixture to a large bowl; add the egg yolk, 60 g (2 oz) of the cheese and some pepper, and mix well. (To purée the vegetables in a food mill, work them once through the mill into a large bowl. Then add the milk, sugar, egg yolk, cheese and pepper, and mix vigorously.)

Preheat the oven to 230°C (450°F or Mark 7). In a clean, dry metal bowl, beat the egg whites just until soft peaks form; do not overbeat them. Fold one quarter of the whites into the carrot mixture and blend well. Fold another quarter of the whites into the courgette mixture and blend well. Gently fold half of the remaining whites into the carrot mixture; the whites should not be completely incorporated. Repeat the process with the remaining egg whites and the courgette mixture.

Remove the soufflé dish from the refrigerator. Pour the two vegetable mixtures simultaneously into opposite sides of the dish. Place a spoon in the middle of the courgette mixture and draw it three quarters of the way around the soufflé to achieve a marbled effect. Sprinkle the remaining cheese over the top. Bake the soufflé for 45 minutes; the top should be golden-brown and puffed up. Serve immediately.

Curried Carrots and Raisins

Serves 6
Working time: about 25 minutes
Total time: about 35 minutes

Calories **95**
Protein **1g**
Cholesterol **5mg**
Total fat **4g**
Saturated fat **1g**
Sodium **35mg**

600 g	carrots, peeled, halved lengthwise, cut diagonally into 1 cm (½ inch) pieces	1¼ lb
1 tbsp	honey	1 tbsp
½ tbsp	fresh lemon juice	½ tbsp
1 tsp	Dijon mustard	1 tsp
1½ tsp	curry powder	1½ tsp
1 tbsp	safflower oil	1 tbsp
7 g	unsalted butter	¼ oz
½ tbsp	brown sugar	½ tbsp
60 g	raisins	2 oz

Pour enough water into a saucepan to fill it 2.5 cm (1 inch) deep. Set a vegetable steamer in the pan and bring the water to the boil. Put the carrots in the steamer, cover the pan, and steam the carrots until they are tender — about 10 minutes. Remove the pan from the heat, uncover it and set it aside.

While the carrots are steaming, combine the honey, lemon juice, mustard and curry powder in a bowl.

Put the oil and butter in a large, heavy frying pan over medium-high heat. When the butter bubbles, add the carrot pieces and sauté them, stirring often, for 2 minutes.

Sprinkle the brown sugar over the carrots, add the raisins, and cook the mixture, stirring constantly, for 2 minutes more. Stir in the honey mixture and continue cooking, stirring constantly and scraping down the sides of the pan, until the carrots are well glazed — 2 or 3 minutes more. Serve at once.

Purée of Carrots and Turnips

Serves 6
Working time: about 20 minutes
Total time: about 40 minutes

Calories **70**
Protein **1g**
Cholesterol **10mg**
Total fat **4g**
Saturated fat **2g**
Sodium **120mg**

500 g	carrots, peeled and sliced into 5 mm (¼ inch) rounds	1 lb
2	turnips, peeled and cut into 1 cm (½ inch) cubes	2
1	large onion, cut lengthwise into 8 wedges	1
6 cl	single cream	2 fl oz
15 g	unsalted butter	½ oz
¼ tsp	salt	¼ tsp
	freshly ground black pepper	

Pour enough water into a large saucepan to fill it about 2.5 cm (1 inch) deep. Set a vegetable steamer in the pan and bring the water to the boil. Put the carrots in the steamer, then cover them with the turnips and the onion. Cover and steam until the carrots are very tender when pierced with the tip of a sharp knife — about 20 minutes.

Purée the vegetables in a food processor for 1 minute. Scrape down the sides, then add the cream, butter, salt and pepper; blend again until the mixture is smooth. (Alternatively, press the vegetables through a sieve set over a bowl. Then add the cream, butter, salt and pepper, and mix vigorously.) Serve immediately.

Beetroot Purée

Serves 4
Working time: about 15 minutes
Total time: about 1 hour and 15 minutes

Calories **70**
Protein **2g**
Cholesterol **0mg**
Total fat **0g**
Saturated fat **0g**
Sodium **190mg**

750 g	beetroots, washed and trimmed, 5 cm (2 inch) stem left on each	1½ lb
1	potato (about 250 g/½ lb)	1
1 tsp	raspberry vinegar or red wine vinegar	1 tsp
⅛ tsp	ground ginger	⅛ tsp
⅛ tsp	grated nutmeg	⅛ tsp
¼ tsp	salt	¼ tsp
	freshly ground black pepper	

Preheat the oven to 200°C (400°F or Mark 6). Wrap the beetroots, in a single package, in aluminium foil. Prick the potato with a fork. Bake the beetroots and the potato until they are tender — about 1 hour.

While the beetroots and the potato are still hot, peel off their skins. Work the vegetables through a food mill or a fine-meshed sieve into a large bowl. (Puréeing the potato in a food processor or blender would make it gluey.) Add the vinegar, ginger, nutmeg, salt and pepper, and mix well with a whisk; transfer the purée to a serving dish. As a decorative touch, the surface of the purée may be indented with the edge of a large spoon. Serve the purée immediately.

Parsnip Purée Spiked with Horseradish

Serves 6
Working time: about 25 minutes
Total time: about 1 hour

Calories **110**
Protein **2g**
Cholesterol **10mg**
Total fat **5g**
Saturated fat **3g**
Sodium **20mg**

850 g	parsnips, peeled and sliced into 5 mm (¼ inch) rounds	1¾ lb
30 g	unsalted butter	1 oz
250 g	cooking apples, peeled, cored and cut into 5 mm (¼ inch) slices	8 oz
¼ litre	unsalted chicken or vegetable stock	8 fl oz
1 tbsp	prepared horseradish	1 tbsp
	white pepper	

In a large, heavy frying pan, melt half of the butter over medium-low heat. Add the parsnips and apple, and pour the stock over them. Cover the pan and cook the mixture until the parsnips are soft — 30 to 35 minutes.

Purée the parsnips, apples and any remaining cooking liquid in a food processor or a food mill. Transfer the mixture to a saucepan and warm it over medium-low heat. Add the remaining butter, the horseradish and white pepper, and stir vigorously. Serve the dish immediately.

Diced Beetroots with Orange and Yogurt Sauce

Serves 4
Working time: about 20 minutes
Total time: about 1 hour and 15 minutes

Calories **50**
Protein **2g**
Cholesterol **5mg**
Total fat **0g**
Saturated fat **0g**
Sodium **115mg**

500 g	beetroots, peeled and cut into 5 mm (¼ inch) cubes	1 lb
6 cl	cider vinegar	2 fl oz
1 tbsp	grated orange rind	1 tbsp
⅛ tsp	ground mace	⅛ tsp
⅛ tsp	ground cloves	⅛ tsp
⅛ tsp	salt	⅛ tsp
	freshly ground black pepper	
6 cl	plain low-fat yogurt	2 fl oz
2 tbsp	fresh orange juice	2 tbsp
1 tsp	honey	1 tsp

Preheat the oven to 190°C (375°F or Mark 5). In a 1.5 litre (2½ pint) ovenproof casserole with a lid, combine the beetroots, vinegar, 6 cl (2 fl oz) of water, orange rind, mace, cloves, salt and pepper. Bake the beetroot mixture, covered, for 1 hour.

Meanwhile, to make the sauce, mix together the yogurt and orange juice in a small bowl. Refrigerate the sauce until ready to serve.

Remove the beetroots from the oven and stir in the honey. Serve immediately, topped with the yogurt sauce.

Swede Pancake

Serves 8
Working time: about 25 minutes
Total time: about 1 hour and 15 minutes

Calories **120**
Protein **2g**
Cholesterol **35mg**
Total fat **6g**
Saturated fat **1g**
Sodium **155mg**

1	small swede (about 600 g/1 ¼ lb), peeled	1
2	medium potatoes, peeled	2
3	spring onions, trimmed and very thinly sliced	3
1 tbsp	cornflour, mixed with 1 tbsp cold water	1 tbsp
1	whole egg, plus 1 egg white, beaten	1
1 tbsp	brown sugar	1 tbsp
½ tsp	salt	½ tsp
¼ tsp	cayenne pepper	¼ tsp
3 tbsp	safflower oil	3 tbsp

Coarsely grate the swede. Firmly squeeze the grated flesh, a handful at a time, over a sink to rid it of excess moisture; as you work, transfer the swede to a large bowl. Grate the potatoes into the bowl, then add the spring onions and stir well to combine the vegetables.

Whisk together the cornflour mixture and the eggs. Stir them into the vegetables with the brown sugar, salt and cayenne pepper. Mix well.

Heat 2 tablespoons of the oil in a large non-stick or well-seasoned Spanish omelette pan, or frying pan with removable handle, over medium-high heat. When the oil is hot, put the vegetable mixture in the pan and quickly flatten it with a spatula to a uniform thickness. Reduce the heat to medium low and cook the pancake until the bottom is golden-brown — 20 to 25 minutes. To flip the pancake, first invert over the pancake a plate larger than the pan. Then turn the pan and plate over together, leaving the pancake on the plate. Preheat the oven to 190°C (375°F or Mark 5).

Heat the remaining tablespoon of oil in the pan over medium heat. Carefully slide the pancake from the plate back into the pan and cook it for 5 minutes. Then put the pan in the oven (removing the handle, if necessary) and bake the pancake until the bottom is golden-brown and the top crisp — about 25 minutes. Gently slide the pancake on to a serving plate, cut it into wedges and serve.

EDITOR'S NOTE: *If you do not have a non-stick pan, increase the amount of oil to 4½ tablespoons; use 3 tablespoons to cook the pancake on the first side, 1½ tablespoons for the second.*

Spring Onions with Red Pepper and Lime

Serves 6
Working (and total) time: about 30 minutes

Calories **105**
Protein **3g**
Cholesterol **0mg**
Total fat **5g**
Saturated fat **1g**
Sodium **65mg**

4	bunches spring onions, trimmed to about 20 cm (8 inches) long	4
¼ litre	unsalted chicken stock	8 fl oz
1	onion, sliced	1
1	garlic clove, chopped	1
1	sweet red pepper, seeded, deribbed and coarsely chopped	1
2 tbsp	virgin olive oil	2 tbsp
⅛ tsp	salt	⅛ tsp
	freshly ground black pepper	
1	lime, cut into 6 slices	1

Combine the stock, onion and garlic in a small saucepan. Cook the mixture over high heat until the liquid is reduced by half — about 5 minutes. Stir in the sweet red pepper, reduce the heat to medium, and simmer until the pepper is tender — about 3 minutes more.

Pour enough water into a large frying pan to fill it about 2.5 cm (1 inch) deep, and bring it to the boil. Cook the spring onions in the water until they are tender — 3 to 4 minutes. Drain them well. To finish the sauce, pour the red pepper mixture into a blender or food processor, and add the oil, salt and black pepper. Purée until smooth — about 1 minute.

Arrange the spring onions on a platter. Spoon some of the sauce over them, garnish with the lime slices and pass the remaining sauce separately.

Stir-Fried Vegetables with Sesame Seeds

Serves 8
Working (and total) time: about 45 minutes

Calories **75**
Protein **4g**
Cholesterol **0mg**
Total fat **4g**
Saturated fat **0g**
Sodium **170mg**

1 tsp	sesame seeds	1 tsp
2 tbsp	low-sodium soy sauce, or naturally fermented shoyu	2 tbsp
1	lime, juice only	1
1 tsp	dry sherry	1 tsp
¼ tsp	honey	¼ tsp
¼ tsp	cayenne pepper	¼ tsp
	freshly ground black pepper	
500 g	broccoli, trimmed, florets cut from stalks and stalks peeled	1 lb
2 tbsp	safflower oil	2 tbsp
2	large shallots, thinly sliced	2
250 g	swedes, peeled, quartered and cut into 5 mm (¼ inch) slices	8 oz
250 g	cauliflower florets	8 oz
1	small carrot, peeled, sliced diagonally	1

Preheat a small, heavy frying pan over medium-low heat. Toast the sesame seeds until they are lightly browned — 8 to 10 minutes. Transfer the seeds to a mortar and crush them with a pestle. (Alternatively, crush the seeds with the flat of a heavy knife.) Stir in the soy sauce, lime juice, sherry, honey, cayenne pepper and black pepper, and set the mixture aside.

To allow the broccoli stalks to absorb more seasoning, use a roll cut to increase their surface area. Cut a diagonal slice off one of the broccoli stalks about 1 cm (½ inch) from its end. Rotate the stalk a quarter turn and cut off another diagonal slice. Continue rotating and cutting until the stalk is completely sliced. Repeat the process with the other stalk and set the slices aside.

Heat a wok or a large, heavy frying pan over high heat for 1 to 2 minutes. Add the oil and tip the pan to coat it evenly. Return the pan to the heat, add the shallots, and stir-fry them for 30 seconds.

Add the swedes and stir-fry for 1 minute. Then pour in 8 cl (3 fl oz) of water. Cover the pan and cook the swedes

until you hear a sizzling sound (an indication that the water is about to evaporate) — about 4 minutes. Add the sliced broccoli stalks, cauliflower florets and carrot slices, and stir-fry the vegetables for 1 minute. Pour another 8 cl (3 fl oz) of water into the pan. Cover the pan and steam the vegetables until they are tender but still crisp — about 3 minutes.

Stir in the broccoli florets and replenish the water if necessary. Re-cover the pan and steam the broccoli florets until they are tender — about 2 minutes. Uncover the pan and continue to cook the mixture, stirring constantly, until the liquid has evaporated. Pour in the sesame-seed mixture and toss the vegetables to coat them well. Serve immediately.

Parsnip, Artichoke and Aubergine Gratin

Serves 8
Working time: about 45 minutes
Total time: about 1 hour and 15 minutes

Calories **135**
Protein **6g**
Cholesterol **15mg**
Total fat **9g**
Saturated fat **3g**
Sodium **195mg**

2	large parsnips, peeled, cut into 1 cm (½ inch) rounds, biggest rounds cut in half	2
½	lemon	½
4	artichoke bottoms (page 13)	4
2	garlic cloves	2
1	medium aubergine (about 350 g/12 oz)	1
1 tbsp	safflower oil	1 tbsp
1 tbsp	virgin olive oil	1 tbsp
¼ tsp	salt	¼ tsp
1 tsp	chopped fresh thyme, or ¼ tsp dried thyme	1 tsp
1 tbsp	finely chopped fresh basil, or 1½ tsp dried basil	1 tbsp
10 g	unsalted butter	⅓ oz
1	onion, chopped	1
60 g	Gruyère cheese, grated	2 oz
60 g	Parmesan cheese, freshly grated	2 oz

In a large non-reactive saucepan, bring 1 litre (1¾ pints) of water to the boil. Squeeze the juice of the lemon into the water and add the lemon itself. Add the artichoke bottoms and boil until tender — 8 to 10 minutes. Remove the artichoke bottoms, cut them into eighths when cool, and set them aside.

Pour enough water into a second saucepan to fill it 2.5 cm (1 inch) deep. Set a vegetable steamer in the pan and bring the water to the boil. Put the parsnip rounds in the steamer, cover the pan, and steam the rounds until they are tender but still somewhat firm — about 4 minutes. Allow them to cool.

Rub the bottom and sides of a baking dish with one half of the garlic clove. Then chop it finely with the rest of the garlic and set the garlic aside.

Preheat the oven to 180°C (350°F or Mark 4). Peel 2.5 cm (1 inch) vertical strips from the aubergine skin to stripe it. Cut the aubergine horizontally into 2 cm (¾ inch) slices, then into 2 cm (¾ inch) cubes. In a heavy frying pan, heat the safflower and olive oils over medium-high heat. Add the aubergine and cook for 3 minutes. Stir in the chopped garlic, half of the salt, the thyme and the basil, and cook until the aubergine is soft — about 3 minutes. Transfer the aubergine mixture to a large bowl. Using the same pan, put in the butter, the onion and the remaining salt, and sauté over medium-low heat until the onion is translucent — about 10 minutes. Remove from the heat.

Combine the artichokes, parsnips and onion with the aubergine. Add the Gruyère and half the Parmesan cheese. Spread the mixture in a baking dish, sprinkle with the remaining Parmesan and bake for 45 minutes.

Three-Tiered Vegetable Terrine

Serves 12
Working time: about 1 hour and 30 minutes
Total time: about 2 hours and 45 minutes

Calories **90**
Protein **6g**
Cholesterol **75mg**
Total fat **5g**
Saturated fat **2g**
Sodium **225mg**

600 g	carrots, peeled and sliced into 5 mm (¼ inch) thick rounds	1 ¼ lb
2	medium onions (about 375 g/¾ lb), chopped	2
1 kg	cauliflower, cored and cut into large florets	2 lb
40 g	unsalted butter	1 ¼ oz
3	eggs	3
4	egg whites	4
¾ tsp	salt	¾ tsp
⅛ tsp	grated nutmeg	⅛ tsp
	freshly ground black pepper	
3 tbsp	freshly grated Parmesan cheese	3 tbsp
3 tbsp	finely chopped shallots	3 tbsp
1 kg	fresh spinach, washed and stemmed	2 lb
2	garlic cloves, chopped	2

Wipe the inside of a 2 litre (3½ pint) rectangular terrine mould with 15 g (½ oz) of the butter. To facilitate unmoulding the cooked terrine, fit a piece of grease-proof paper in the bottom of the mould and butter it as well. Put the mould in the refrigerator.

Pour enough water into a large, non-reactive sauce-pan to fill it about 2.5 cm (1 inch) deep. Put a vegetable steamer in the pan and bring the water to the boil. Add the carrots and put one third of the onions on top of them. Cover the pan tightly and cook the vegetables until very tender — 16 to 18 minutes. Drain the vegetables on paper towels for 1 minute, then reserve them in a bowl.

Replenish the water in the pan and bring it to the boil. Put the cauliflower in the steamer; layer half the remaining onions on top. Cover the pan and steam the vege-tables until the cauliflower stems are tender — about 20 minutes. Drain the vegetables on paper towels for 1 minute; set them aside in a separate bowl.

Put one of the whole eggs and two of the egg whites into a food processor or blender. Process the eggs for 30 seconds. Add the steamed carrots and onions, ¼ tea-spoon of the salt, the nutmeg and some pepper. Process for about 1 minute, stopping after 30 seconds to scrape down the sides.

Transfer the carrot purée to the chilled mould, smoothing the top with a rubber spatula. Take care not to leave any carrot on the sides of the mould, lest orange spots blemish the finished terrine.

Put another egg and one egg white in the food pro-

cessor and blend them for 30 seconds. Add the steamed cauliflower and onions, the cheese, shallots, ¼ teaspoon of the salt and some pepper; process for about 1 minute, stopping after 30 seconds to scrape down the sides.

Transfer the cauliflower purée to the mould, spread-ing it in an even layer over the carrot purée. Preheat the oven to 180°C (350°F or Mark 4).

Prepare a water bath: place the terrine mould in a large baking dish — preferably one that is at least 5 cm (2 inches) larger than the mould all round — and pour enough hot water into the dish to come two thirds of the way up the sides of the mould. Remove the mould and set the baking dish in the oven.

Pour out any water remaining in the pan and then pour in just enough fresh water to cover the bottom. Set the pan over high heat, add the spinach, and cover. After 3 minutes, remove the pan from the heat and stir the spinach until it is wilted. Drain the spinach and refresh it under cold running water. Form part of the spinach into a ball and firmly squeeze out the liquid with your hands; set the squeezed spinach aside. Repeat the process with the remaining spinach.

Put the remaining butter in a large, heavy frying pan over medium heat. Add the remaining onions and the garlic, and cook for 3 minutes. Stir in the spinach and sprinkle with the remaining salt and a dash of pepper. Remove the pan from the heat.

Put the remaining egg and egg white in the food pro-cessor and blend them for 30 seconds. Transfer the con-tents of the frying pan to the food processor and process for about 1 minute, stopping after 30 seconds to scrape down the sides.

Distribute spoonfuls of the spinach mixture over the layer of cauliflower in the mould, then smooth the top with the rubber spatula, filling the corners without dis-rupting the layer below.

To keep the top from drying out during cooking, cover the spinach with a second piece of buttered greaseproof paper. Set the mould in the water bath in the oven and bake it for 1 hour and 10 minutes.

Remove the terrine from the oven and let it stand for 20 minutes. To unmould it, first run a knife around the insides of the mould to loosen the terrine. Then remove the greaseproof paper from the top and invert a platter larger than the mould over the terrine. Turn mould and plate over together, then carefully lift away the mould and peel off the other piece of greaseproof paper. Allow the terrine to cool slightly — about 5 minutes; then cut it into serving slices, catching each slice on a spatula as you cut it to keep it from breaking apart.

Vegetable Couscous

Serves 8 as a main dish
Working time: about 35 minutes
Total time: about 1 hour

Calories **215**
Protein **9g**
Cholesterol **5mg**
Total fat **5g**
Saturated fat **2g**
Sodium **345mg**

4	tomatoes, skinned and seeded (page 84)	4
1.25 litres	unsalted chicken or vegetable stock	2 pints
2	medium onions, peeled and cut into 2.5 cm (1 inch) pieces	2
2	carrots, peeled and cut diagonally into 1 cm (½ inch) ovals	2
¾ tsp	salt	¾ tsp
25 g	fresh coriander or parsley leaves	¾ oz
350 g	courgettes, quartered lengthwise and cut into 5 cm (2 inch) lengths	12 oz
1	medium turnip, peeled and cut into 2 cm (¾ inch) pieces	1
½	hot green chili pepper, seeded, rinsed and finely chopped	½
30 g	unsalted butter	1 oz
350 g	couscous	12 oz

Chop half of the tomatoes into 2.5 cm (1 inch) pieces and set them aside. Purée the remaining tomatoes in a food processor or blender. Transfer the purée to a large heavy pan, and add ½ litre (16 fl oz) of the stock. Heat the mixture over medium heat. Then add the onions, carrots, ¼ teaspoon of the salt and the corian-der or parsley. Simmer, stirring occasionally, for 10 minutes.

Stir in the courgettes, turnip, the tomato pieces, chili pepper and ¼ teaspoon of the salt. Partially cover the pan, leaving a 2.5 cm (1 inch) opening to vent the steam, and cook the mixture for 30 minutes more.

Meanwhile, pour the remaining stock into a large, heavy pan with tight-fitting lid. Stir in the butter and the remaining salt; bring the liquid to a rolling boil. Stir in the couscous and cook it stirring constantly, for 30 seconds. Remove from the heat, cover and let it stand for 7 minutes, then transfer it to a serving dish and fluff it with a fork.

To serve, divide the couscous among individual bowls. Spoon some vegetables and broth over each serving.

Chili Peppers — a Cautionary Note

Both dried and fresh hot chili peppers should be handled with care. Their flesh and seeds contain volatile oils that can make skin tingle and cause eyes to burn. Rubber gloves offer protection — but the cook should still be careful not to touch the face, lips or eyes when working with chilies.

Soaking fresh chilies in cold, salted water for an hour will remove some of their fire. If canned chilies are substituted for fresh ones, they should be rinsed in cold water in order to eliminate as much of the brine used to preserve them as possible.

Onions Stuffed with Spinach and Pine-Nuts

Serves 6
Working time: about 45 minutes
Total time: about 1 hour and 10 minutes

Calories **110**
Protein **5g**
Cholesterol **5mg**
Total fat **4g**
Saturated fat **0g**
Sodium **130mg**

6	medium onions (about 850 g/1¾ lb)	6
45 g	currants	1½ oz
½ tsp	safflower oil	½ tsp
1	garlic clove, finely chopped	1
500 g	spinach, washed and stemmed	1 lb
¼ tsp	salt	¼ tsp
12.5 cl	plain low-fat yogurt	4 fl oz
25 g	pine-nuts, toasted	¾ oz
1 tbsp	orange rind	1 tbsp
⅛ tsp	grated nutmeg	⅛ tsp
2 tbsp	fresh wholemeal breadcrumbs	2 tbsp

Level the bottoms of the onions by trimming the root end off each one (take care not to remove too much, lest the onions lose their shape while cooking). Discard the ends and peel the onions. Cut a 1 cm (½ inch) slice off the top of each onion and set the tops aside. With a melon baller or a grapefruit spoon, hollow out the onions, forming shells with walls approximately 1 cm (½ inch) thick. Reserve the scooped-out centres.

Pour enough water into a saucepan to fill it about 2.5 cm (1 inch) deep. Set a vegetable steamer in the pan and bring the water to the boil. Put the onion shells in the steamer, cover the pan, and steam the shells until they are tender when pierced with the tip of a knife — 10 to 15 minutes. Set the shells aside.

Meanwhile, put the currants in a small bowl and pour in just enough water to cover them. Set the bowl aside to allow the currants to plump.

Finely chop the onion tops and centres. In a large, heavy frying pan, heat the oil over medium-low heat. Add the chopped onion and garlic and cook, stirring occasionally, until the onion is soft but not browned — 5 to 7 minutes.

Add the spinach, cover the pan, and cook until the spinach is wilted — about 3 minutes. Uncover the pan, add the salt, and cook the mixture, stirring occasionally, until all the liquid has evaporated — 5 to 7 minutes more. Transfer the onion-spinach mixture to a large bowl and let it cool.

Preheat the oven to 180°C (350°F or Mark 4). Drain the currants and add them to the onion-spinach mixture. Add the yogurt, pine-nuts, rind and nutmeg, and mix well. Pour out and discard any liquid that has accumulated in the onion shells, and spoon some stuffing into them.

Spread the remaining stuffing on the bottom of a small baking dish; set the filled onion shells on the stuffing. Sprinkle the breadcrumbs over the top of the stuffed onions and bake the onions for 20 to 25 minutes. Remove the baking dish from the oven and preheat the grill. Grill the onions just long enough to crisp the breadcrumbs. Serve the onions with a little stuffing from the bottom of the dish spooned beside each portion.

bined but not foamy. Transfer the onion mixture to a food processor or blender and purée it, gradually pouring in the saffron-flavoured stock as you work. Pour this mixture into the beaten eggs, add a pinch of cayenne pepper, and beat until just mixed. Butter a ¾ litre (1¼ pint) mould, pour the mixture into it, and cover the top with foil. Set the mould in a deep baking dish and pour in enough boiling water to come half way up the sides of the mould. Bake the timbale until it sets — 40 to 50 minutes.

Remove the mould from the water bath and let it stand for 10 minutes. In the meantime, warm the sauce over low heat. Remove the foil from the mould, run a knife around the inside edge and unmould the timbale on to a heated serving dish. Pour the red pepper sauce around the border and garnish the timbale with the remaining spring onions.

EDITOR'S NOTE: *To give body and texture to the timbale, the chicken stock must be rich and gelatinous. Four small ramekins may be used instead of the large mould, provided the cooking time is reduced to 20 to 25 minutes.*

Onion Timbale with Red Pepper Sauce

A TIMBALE IS A CREAMY VEGETABLE MIXTURE BAKED IN A MOULD.

Serves 4
Working time: about 30 minutes
Total time: about 1 hour and 30 minutes

Calories **100**
Protein **5g**
Cholesterol **70mg**
Total fat **6g**
Saturated fat **1g**
Sodium **215mg**

275 g	onion, coarsely chopped	9 oz
1 tbsp	virgin olive oil	1 tbsp
45 g	finely chopped green spring onion tops	1½ oz
¼ tsp	salt	¼ tsp
¼ litre	gelatinous unsalted chicken stock	8 fl oz
⅛ tsp	saffron threads	⅛ tsp
1	whole egg, plus 2 egg whites	1
	cayenne pepper	
	Red pepper sauce	
2	sweet red peppers, grilled and peeled (page 72)	2
12.5 cl	unsalted chicken stock	4 fl oz
	cayenne pepper	

Heat the oil in a heavy frying pan over low heat. Add the onion, all but 2 tablespoons of the spring onions and the salt. Cook the mixture until the onion becomes very soft — 15 to 20 minutes. Remove the pan from the heat and allow the mixture to cool.

While the onion is cooking, make the sauce. Remove the stems and seeds from the peppers. Purée the peppers in a food processor or blender. Transfer the purée to a saucepan, pour in the stock, and sprinkle with a pinch of cayenne pepper. Set the pan aside. Preheat the oven to 180°C (350°F or Mark 4).

Warm the gelatinous stock over low heat and dissolve the saffron threads in it. In a mixing bowl, lightly beat the egg and egg whites until they are just com-

Onion and Goat Cheese Pizza

Serves 8
Working time: about 40 minutes
Total time: about 2 hours and 30 minutes

Calories **220**
Protein **6g**
Cholesterol **10mg**
Total fat **10g**
Saturated fat **3g**
Sodium **170mg**

1.5 kg	onions, thinly sliced	3 lb
2 tbsp	virgin olive oil	2 tbsp
2 tsp	fresh thyme, or ½ tsp dried thyme	2 tsp
6 cl	red wine vinegar or cider vinegar	2 fl oz
¼ tsp	salt	¼ tsp
1 tbsp	cornmeal	1 tbsp
90 g	mild goat cheese or feta cheese	3 oz
60 g	low-fat cream cheese	2 oz
	Thyme-flavoured pizza dough	
7 g	dried yeast	¼ oz
¼ tsp	sugar	¼ tsp
250 g	strong plain flour	8 oz
¼ tsp	salt	¼ tsp
2 tsp	fresh thyme, or ½ tsp dried thyme	2 tsp
2 tbsp	virgin olive oil	2 tbsp

To make the dough, pour 12.5 cl (4 fl oz) lukewarm water into a small bowl and sprinkle the yeast and sugar into it. Let the mixture stand for 2 to 3 minutes, then stir it until the yeast and sugar are completely dissolved. Allow the mixture to stand in a warm place until the yeast bubbles up and the mixture has doubled in bulk — about 15 minutes.

Sift 200 g (7 oz) of the flour and the salt into a large bowl, and stir in the thyme. Make a well in the centre and pour in the yeast mixture and the oil. Mix the dough by hand; it should feel slightly sticky. If it feels too sticky, work in some, or all, of the remaining flour;

if it is too dry, add a little more water. As soon as the dough is firm enough to be gathered into a ball, place it on a floured board and knead it until it is smooth and elastic — about 10 minutes.

Put the dough in a clean oiled bowl and cover it with a damp towel. Set the bowl in a warm, draught-free place until the dough has doubled in bulk — about 1 to 1½ hours.

While the dough is rising, make the onion topping. Heat 1 tablespoon of the olive oil in a large, heavy-bottomed fireproof casserole over medium heat. Put the onions and thyme in the casserole and cook them, stirring and scraping the bottom frequently, until the onions are well browned — 45 minutes to 1 hour. Add the vinegar and salt, and cook, stirring often, until the liquid has evaporated — about 10 minutes.

Preheat the oven to 230°C (450°F or Mark 8). Sprinkle the cornmeal on a large, heavy baking sheet. Knock down the dough, then gather it up into a ball and flatten it with your hands. Stretch out the dough by holding it at the edges with both hands and turning it until it forms a circle about 20 cm (8 inches) in diameter. Put the circle in the centre of the baking sheet and pat it out to 30 cm (12 inches) in diameter.

Distribute the onions in an even layer over the pizza dough, leaving a 1 cm (½ inch) border uncovered at the edge. Combine the goat or feta cheese and the cream cheese in a small bowl; dot the pizza with the cheese mixture. Bake the pizza for 10 minutes. Remove it from the oven and dribble the remaining oil ▶

over the top. Return the pizza to the oven and bake it until the bottom of the crust is browned and the cheese turns golden — 4 to 6 minutes. Cut the pizza into wedges and serve at once.

EDITOR'S NOTE: *To prepare the pizza dough in a food processor, put 200 g (7 oz) of the flour, the salt and thyme in the processor and mix it in two short bursts. In a separate small mixing bowl, combine the bubbling yeast mixture with the oil. While the motor is running, pour the mixture into the processor as fast as the flour will absorb it; process until a ball of dough comes away from the sides of the bowl — about 1 minute. If the dough is too sticky to form a ball, work in up to 30 g (1 oz) additional flour; if too dry, add a little water. Remove the dough from the processor, place it on a floured board and knead it for 5 minutes. Set the dough aside to rise as described above.*

Leeks and Cheese in Phyllo Packets

Serves 6
Working time: about 45 minutes
Total time: about 1 hour and 45 minutes

Calories **275**
Protein **9g**
Cholesterol **30mg**
Total fat **14g**
Saturated fat **6g**
Sodium **290mg**

4	medium leeks, trimmed, cleaned (below), sliced into 1 cm (½ inch) pieces	4
1 tbsp	safflower oil	1 tbsp
30 g	unsalted butter	1 oz
275 g	onion, chopped	9 oz
1	garlic clove, finely chopped	1
½ tsp	dried thyme	½ tsp
¼ tsp	salt	¼ tsp
	freshly ground black pepper	
2 tbsp	single cream	2 tbsp
150 g	Gruyère or other Swiss cheese, grated	5 oz
12	sheets phyllo pastry, each 30 cm (12 inches) square	12

In a large, heavy frying pan, heat the oil and half the butter over medium heat. Add the leeks, onion, garlic, thyme, salt and pepper. Cook, stirring often, for 12 minutes. Stir in the cream and continue cooking until all the liquid is absorbed — about 3 minutes more.

Transfer the leek mixture to a bowl and let it cool slightly. Stir in the cheese and refrigerate the mixture for 30 minutes.

Preheat the oven to 180°C (350°F or Mark 4). On a clean, dry work surface, lay out two sheets of phyllo dough, one on top of the other. Mound about one sixth of the leek-cheese mixture 7.5 cm (3 inches) from the lower right corner of the dough. Fold up the dough as shown on the right, forming a compact packet. Repeat the process with the remaining filling and dough sheets to form six packets in all. Put the packets, seam sides down, on a lightly buttered baking sheet. Melt the remaining butter in a small saucepan over low heat. Brush the packets with the melted butter and bake them until they are golden — about 30 minutes. Serve them hot.

EDITOR'S NOTE: *These make an excellent luncheon dish served with a green salad. Thaw frozen phyllo before using.*

Cleaning Leeks

1 *SPLITTING THE LEEK. Remove any bruised outer leaves from the leek. Cut off the root base and the tough leaf tops. With a paring knife, pierce the leek about 5 cm (2 inches) below the green portion, then draw the knife through to the top to split the leek.*

2 *RINSING OUT THE GRIT. Dip the leafy part of the leek into a bowl of water and swirl it vigorously to flush out the grit. Alternatively, rinse well under running water. Run your fingers along the insides of the leaves to remove any remaining particles of sand.*

Forming a Phyllo Packet

1 *MAKING THE FIRST FOLD.* Spread out two sheets of phyllo one on top of the other. Place the filling in a mound 7.5 cm (3 inches) from the lower right corner. Fold the corner over until it touches the far edge of the filling.

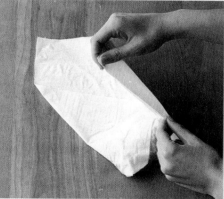

2 *FOLDING IN THE SIDES.* Lift the lower left corner of the phyllo square and fold it towards the centre of the square. Repeat the procedure with the upper right corner so that the filling is enclosed on both sides.

3 *ROLLING THE PACKET.* Gently roll the enclosed filling towards the far corner of the dough square to form a compact parcel. Set the packet aside; repeat the process with the remaining filling and phyllo sheets to form six packets in all.

Leek Pie

Serves 6
Working time: about 40 minutes
Total time: about 1 hour

Calories **250**
Protein **9g**
Cholesterol **15mg**
Total fat **8g**
Saturated fat **3g**
Sodium **145mg**

1 kg	potatoes, peeled	2½ lb
4 to 5 tbsp	skimmed milk	4 to 5 tbsp
75 g	Gruyère cheese, finely grated	2½ oz
	freshly ground black pepper	
750 g	leeks, trimmed and washed thoroughly	1½ lb
1	large onion, thinly sliced	1
1 tbsp	virgin olive oil	1 tbsp
¼ tsp	salt	¼ tsp
2 tsp	mixed dried herbs	2 tsp
About 30 cl	unsalted chicken stock or skimmed milk	About ½ pint
15 g	unsalted butter	½ oz
15 g	plain flour	½ oz

Cut the potatoes into quarters, then steam them until cooked through — about 25 to 30 minutes. Mash the cooked potatoes well, beat in the milk and cheese and season with pepper. Put the potatoes into a large piping bag fitted with a large star nozzle and pipe an attractive border round the inside edge of a fireproof dish.

Cut the leeks into 1 cm (½ inch) thick slices. Heat the oil in a large shallow saucepan, then add the leeks, onion, salt and herbs. Cover the pan with a tightly fitting lid and cook gently until the leeks are just tender, shaking the pan frequently during cooking — 25 to 30 minutes. Strain the juices from the leeks and make them up to 30 cl (½ pint) with chicken stock or milk. Set the leeks aside.

Melt the butter in the saucepan, add the flour, and stir in the leek juices and stock or milk. Bring slowly to the boil, stirring all the time until the sauce thickens. Return the leeks to the pan, reduce the heat and simmer gently for 5 minutes.

Brown the piped potato border under a hot grill, then pour the leeks into the centre. Serve immediately.

SUGGESTED ACCOMPANIMENT: *sliced tomatoes with chives.*

Sherry-Glazed Turnips

Serves 6
Working time: about 20 minutes
Total time: about 45 minutes

Calories **60**
Protein **2g**
Cholesterol **5mg**
Total fat **1g**
Saturated fat **0g**
Sodium **160mg**

1 kg	small turnips, peeled	2 lb
1 litre	unsalted chicken stock	1¾ pints
¼ tsp	salt	¼ tsp
	freshly ground black pepper	
6 cl	cream sherry	2 fl oz
1 tbsp	chopped parsley	1 tbsp

Put the turnips in a heavy frying pan large enough to hold them in one layer. Pour in the stock; add the salt and pepper. Bring the liquid to the boil, then reduce the heat to medium and cook the mixture until almost all of the stock has evaporated — about 15 minutes.

Pour in the remaining stock, bring it to the boil, and cook as before until hardly any remains. Add the sherry and cook until just enough remains to form a sauce — about 3 minutes more. Transfer the turnips to a dish and sprinkle them with the parsley.

Julienned Turnips
in a Warm Vinaigrette

Serves 4
Working (and total) time: about 20 minutes

Calories **40**
Protein **1g**
Cholesterol **0mg**
Total fat **1g**
Saturated fat **0g**
Sodium **95mg**

350 g	turnips, peeled and julienned	12 oz
3 tbsp	fresh lime juice	3 tbsp
1 tbsp	raspberry or red wine vinegar	1 tbsp
1 tsp	virgin olive oil	1 tsp
½ tsp	honey	½ tsp
½ tsp	ground coriander	½ tsp
⅛ tsp	salt	⅛ tsp
	freshly ground black pepper	
125 g	courgettes, julienned	4 oz
30 g	radishes, sliced	1 oz

To prepare the vinaigrette, combine the lime juice, vinegar, oil, honey, coriander, salt and pepper in a small saucepan. Warm the vinaigrette over low heat while you prepare the vegetables.

Pour enough water into a large saucepan to fill it about 2.5 cm (1 inch) deep. Set a vegetable steamer in the pan and bring the water to the boil. Add the turnips and steam them for about 1 minute. Then add the courgettes and radishes, and steam them until all of the vegetables are soft but not limp — about 1 minute more. Transfer the vegetables to a serving dish.

Bring the vinaigrette just to the boil and pour it over the vegetables. Toss well and serve at once.

Baked Garlic Sautéed with Mushrooms and Spring Onions

OLDER BUTTON MUSHROOMS — THOSE WITH EXPOSED GILLS —
ARE SPECIFIED HERE BECAUSE OF THEIR RELATIVELY LOW
MOISTURE CONTENT AND PRONOUNCED FLAVOUR.

Serves 4
Working time: about 25 minutes
Total time: about 1 hour and 30 minutes

Calories **110**
Protein **3g**
Cholesterol **0mg**
Total fat **7g**
Saturated fat **1g**
Sodium **150mg**

2	large garlic bulbs, papery tops cut off to expose the cloves	2
6 tsp	virgin olive oil	6 tsp
¼ tsp	salt	¼ tsp
300 g	button mushrooms (with gills exposed), wiped clean and thinly sliced	10 oz
1 tsp	fresh thyme, or ¼ tsp dried thyme	1 tsp
	freshly ground black pepper	
6	spring onions, trimmed, green tops cut into 2.5 cm (1 inch) lengths, white bottoms halved lengthwise	6

Preheat the oven to 180°C (350°F or Mark 4). With the

palm of your hand, press down lightly on the top of each garlic bulb to loosen the cloves. Place the bulbs in a small, ovenproof baking dish. Dribble 1 teaspoon of the oil over the exposed cloves, then sprinkle ⅛ teaspoon of the salt over them. Bake the garlic bulbs for 45 minutes.

Remove the dish from the oven and dribble another teaspoon of oil over the cloves. Return the dish to the oven and bake until the cloves are golden-brown on top — about 30 minutes more. Then let the garlic bulbs stand for about 10 minutes; when they are cool enough to handle, remove the cloves from their skins and set them aside.

Add the remaining oil and the salt and oil from the baking dish to a large, heavy frying pan over medium-high heat. When the oil is hot, add the mushrooms, the thyme, the remaining salt and the pepper; sauté the mixture, stirring frequently, until the liquid from the mushrooms has evaporated and the mushrooms begin to brown — 3 to 4 minutes. Add the garlic cloves and spring onion bottoms to the pan and cook them, stirring frequently, for 3 minutes. Toss in the spring onion tops and cook the garlic mixture for 2 minutes more. Serve immediately.

Celeriac Gratin

Serves 8
Working time: about 30 minutes
Total time: about 45 minutes

Calories **105**
Protein **5g**
Cholesterol **10mg**
Total fat **5g**
Saturated fat **2g**
Sodium **230mg**

1 kg	celeriac, scrubbed well	2 lb
1	lemon	1
12.5 cl	unsalted chicken or vegetable stock	4 fl oz
1 tbsp	safflower oil	1 tbsp
2	spring onions, trimmed and chopped	2
2 tbsp	flour	2 tbsp
12.5 cl	skimmed milk	4 fl oz
60 g	Gruyère cheese, grated	2 oz
⅛ tsp	grated nutmeg	⅛ tsp
¼ tsp	salt	¼ tsp
⅛ tsp	white pepper	⅛ tsp
2 tbsp	freshly grated Parmesan cheese	2 tbsp
1 tsp	paprika	1 tsp

Squeeze the juice of the lemon into a large bowl of cold water. Peel the celeriac and cut each one into 5 mm (¼ inch) slices. To keep them from discolouring, drop the slices into the acidulated water as you work.

Drain the slices and place them in a fireproof gratin dish. Pour the stock over the celeriac and cover the dish with aluminium foil. Bring the stock to a simmer over medium heat and cook the celeriac until it is tender — 10 to 12 minutes.

Preheat the grill. To prepare the sauce, first heat the oil in a small saucepan over medium heat, then add the spring onions and cook them until they are soft — 2 to 3 minutes. Whisk in the flour, cook for 1 minute, then whisk in the milk. Tip the gratin dish at a slight angle and spoon any cooking liquid into the saucepan. Cook the mixture, whisking constantly, until it thickens — approximately 1 minute. Stir in the Gruyère cheese, nutmeg, salt and pepper. Pour the sauce over the celeriac. Scatter the Parmesan cheese on the top and sprinkle with the paprika. Grill the dish until the top turns golden — 1 to 2 minutes. Serve the celeriac straight from the gratin dish.

Steamed Daikon Radish with Carrot

A DAIKON IS A LONG WHITE JAPANESE RADISH.

Serves 6
Working time: about 30 minutes
Total time: about 40 minutes

Calories **25**
Protein **1g**
Cholesterol **0mg**
Total fat **1g**
Saturated fat **0g**
Sodium **60mg**

500 g	daikon radishes, peeled and julienned	1 lb
15 cl	cider vinegar	¼ pint
¼ tsp	dried thyme leaves	¼ tsp
2	bay leaves	2
12	black peppercorns, cracked	12
1	small carrot, peeled and julienned	1
1	spring onion, trimmed and julienned	1
⅛ tsp	salt	⅛ tsp
¼ tsp	dark sesame oil	¼ tsp

In a small saucepan, combine the vinegar, thyme, bay leaves, peppercorns and 8 cl (3 fl oz) of water. Bring the liquid to the boil and cook until it is reduced to approximately 2 tablespoons — about 5 minutes.

Meanwhile, pour enough water into a saucepan to fill it about 2.5 cm (1 inch) deep. Set a vegetable steamer in the pan and bring the water to the boil. Put the radishes, carrot and spring onion in the steamer. Cover the pan and steam the vegetables until the radishes are tender but still crisp — about 5 minutes. Transfer the vegetables to a serving dish.

Strain the vinegar mixture over the vegetables. Add the salt and oil, and toss well. Serve immediately.

Orange-Glazed Radishes

Serves 6
Working (and total) time: about 25 minutes

Calories **40**
Protein **1g**
Cholesterol **5mg**
Total fat **2g**
Saturated fat **1g**
Sodium **60mg**

500 g	radishes, stem and root ends trimmed	1 lb
1	orange	1
15 g	unsalted butter	½ oz
⅛ tsp	salt	⅛ tsp
	freshly ground black pepper	

Pour enough water into a large saucepan to fill it about 2.5 cm (1 inch) deep. Set a vegetable steamer in the pan and bring the water to the boil. Put the radishes in the steamer and cover the pan. Steam the radishes until they are tender on the outside but still slightly crisp at the centre — 13 to 15 minutes.

While the radishes are steaming, use a small, sharp knife to pare long strips of rind from the orange. Chop the rind very finely and reserve 1 tablespoon of it. Squeeze the juice from the orange into a small bowl.

Melt the butter in a large, heavy frying pan over medium heat. Add the orange juice to the pan and simmer it with the butter until the liquid is syrupy — 2 to 3 minutes.

Transfer the radishes to the pan and sprinkle them with the salt and pepper. Raise the heat to medium high and sauté the radishes until they are evenly coated with a shiny glaze — 2 to 3 minutes. Stir in the reserved rind and cook the mixture for 1 minute more. Serve immediately.

Jerusalem Artichokes with Sautéed Onion

Serves 6
Working time: about 30 minutes
Total time: about 45 minutes

Calories **80**
Protein **2g**
Cholesterol **10mg**
Total fat **3g**
Saturated fat **2g**
Sodium **90mg**

500 g	Jerusalem artichokes, scrubbed well	1 lb
1	lemon	1
25 g	unsalted butter	¾ oz
1	large onion, sliced	1
30 g	finely diced sweet green pepper	1 oz
30 g	finely diced sweet red pepper	1 oz
¼ tsp	salt	¼ tsp
⅛ tsp	white pepper	⅛ tsp

Squeeze the juice of the lemon into a saucepan filled with 1 litre (1¾ pints) of water. Peel the artichokes and cut them into bite-sized pieces, dropping them into the acidulated water to prevent discoloration. Place the pan over high heat; when the water reaches the boil, cook the artichokes until tender but still crisp — about 3 minutes. Drain them and set them aside.

Melt 15 g (½ oz) of the butter in a large, heavy frying pan over medium-high heat. Sauté the sliced onion, stirring occasionally, until it turns golden-brown — about 12 minutes. Reduce the heat to medium, add the diced peppers and the remaining butter, and cook the vegetables for 2 minutes more. Add the artichokes and cook them until they are heated through — about 2 minutes. Stir in the salt and pepper, and serve.

*5*Cauliflower glows golden in a curry sauce tinged with tomato (recipe, opposite). The vegetables and sauce were prepared together in a microwave oven.

Microwaving for Flavour and Health

The newest way of cooking vegetables is also one of the best nutritionally. Besides speeding up the cooking process, microwaving helps to preserve colour, shape and texture. Even better, it ensures that vegetables will retain more of their nutrients than with conventional cooking methods. Often requiring no more additional water than the droplets clinging to them after washing, vegetables literally cook in their own juices and the steam that is trapped in the cooking container when it is covered with a lid or plastic film. Little of the vegetables' vitamin and mineral content can thus be dissolved, and the rapid cooking restricts the destruction of heat-sensitive vitamins.

A wide range of vegetables — from beetroots, broccoli, sweetcorn, potatoes and turnips, to the less familiar kohlrabi, okra and custard marrows — are microwaved in this section. Among the 15 recipes are two quick and easy pickles that will enhance almost any home-cooked meal or family feast. These pickles should be made only in small quantities and stored in the refrigerator. As an added feature, instructions are given for drying herbs in the microwave oven.

When using plastic film to cover a dish containing liquid, one corner should be left open, or the film pricked with a fork, to allow steam to escape; otherwise the build-up of steam may cause the film to explode.

The recipes have been tested in 625-watt and 700-watt ovens. Though power settings vary among different ovens, the recipes use "high" to indicate 100 per cent power. Because it is all too easy to overcook a dish — especially a vegetable dish — in the microwave oven, use the shortest time specified. The dish will go on cooking after it comes out of the oven; always let food stand before testing for doneness. If it needs further cooking, pop it back into the oven.

Cauliflower in Tomato-Curry Sauce

Serves 6
Working time: about 15 minutes
Total time: about 25 minutes

Calories **90**
Protein **4g**
Cholesterol **10mg**
Total fat **5g**
Saturated fat **2g**
Sodium **105mg**

1 kg	cauliflower, trimmed and divided into small florets	2 lb
30 g	unsalted butter	1 oz
2	tomatoes, skinned, seeded (page 84) and chopped	2
1 tsp	curry powder	1 tsp
¼ tsp	finely chopped fresh chili pepper (caution, page 106)	¼ tsp
¼ tsp	grated nutmeg	¼ tsp
⅛ tsp	mustard seeds, crushed	⅛ tsp
¼ tsp	salt	¼ tsp
1	small carrot, peeled and cut into 5 mm (¼ inch) rounds	1
1	small onion, cut into 1 cm (½ inch) cubes	1
45 g	fresh or frozen peas	1½ oz

To prepare the sauce, put the butter in a shallow 2 litre (3½ pint) dish and microwave it on high for 30 seconds to melt it. Remove the dish from the oven and stir in the tomatoes, curry powder, chili pepper, nutmeg, mustard seeds and salt. Add the carrot rounds and toss them with the tomato sauce. Cover the dish with plastic film and microwave it on high for 2 minutes. Add the cauliflower and onion, and toss the vegetables to coat them well with the sauce.

Cover the dish and microwave it on high for 4 minutes. Then stir the vegetables, cover again, and cook on high until the cauliflower and carrots are tender but still crisp — 4 to 5 minutes. Stir in the peas and microwave on high, covered, for 1 minute more. Allow the dish to stand for 2 to 3 minutes before serving.

Garlicky Potato Fans

Serves 4
Working time: about 10 minutes
Total time: about 30 minutes

Calories **165**
Protein **3g**
Cholesterol **0mg**
Total fat **7g**
Saturated fat **1g**
Sodium **140mg**

4	medium potatoes (about 1 kg/2 lb), scrubbed	4
6	garlic cloves, finely chopped	6
1 tsp	dried oregano	1 tsp
2 tbsp	finely chopped parsley	2 tbsp
2 tbsp	virgin olive oil	2 tbsp
¼ tsp	salt	¼ tsp
	freshly ground black pepper	

Combine the garlic, oregano, parsley, oil, salt and pepper in a small bowl. Slice the potatoes almost all the way through, as you would prepare a loaf of garlic bread, making the cuts about 5 mm (¼ inch) apart.

Spread a small amount of garlic mixture inside each cut. Wrap the potatoes in strong plastic film pierced with a fork and microwave them on high, turning them every 4 minutes, until they are tender — 12 to 16 minutes.

Let the potatoes stand for 5 minutes before unwrapping them. Arrange them in a serving dish and press down lightly on each one to fan out the slices.

EDITOR'S NOTE: *To prepare these garlicky potatoes in a conventional oven, wrap them in aluminium foil and bake them for about 1 hour at 200°C (400°F or Mark 6).*

Minted Beetroots

Serves 4
Working time: about 20 minutes
Total time: about 30 minutes

Calories **70**
Protein **2g**
Cholesterol **0mg**
Total fat **1g**
Saturated fat **0g**
Sodium **105mg**

500 g	beetroots, peeled and cut into 1 cm (½ inch) cubes	1 lb
1	onion, finely chopped	1
1	tart apple, peeled, cored, finely chopped	1
⅛ tsp	grated nutmeg	⅛ tsp
⅛ tsp	salt	⅛ tsp
	freshly ground black pepper	
2 tbsp	chopped fresh mint, or 1 tbsp dried mint	2 tbsp
1 tbsp	chopped walnuts	1 tbsp

In a baking dish, combine all the ingredients except the walnuts. Cover tightly and microwave on high, stirring every 2 minutes, until the beetroots are tender — 6 to 8 minutes. Sprinkle the walnuts over the minted beetroots and serve the dish hot or at room temperature.

Brussels Sprouts with Pimiento and Olive Sauce

Serves 6
Working time: about 15 minutes
Total time: about 20 minutes

Calories **100**
Protein **8g**
Cholesterol **5mg**
Total fat **4g**
Saturated fat **2g**
Sodium **85mg**

750 g	Brussels sprouts, trimmed and halved lengthwise	1½ lb
15 g	unsalted butter	½ oz
1 tbsp	flour	1 tbsp
12.5 cl	unsalted chicken or vegetable stock	4 fl oz
2 tsp	brown sugar	2 tsp
1½ tsp	chopped fresh oregano, or ½ tsp dried oregano	1½ tsp
1 tsp	chopped fresh basil, or ½ tsp dried basil	1 tsp
25 g	pimiento strips	¾ oz
3	large black olives, stoned and sliced	3
2 tbsp	freshly grated Parmesan cheese	2 tbsp

Put the Brussels sprouts and 6 cl (2 fl oz) of water in a dish. Cover the dish with plastic film, leaving one corner open, and microwave the sprouts on high until they are just tender — 7 to 9 minutes. Set the sprouts aside.

To prepare the sauce, put the butter in a glass bowl and microwave it on high for 30 seconds. Whisk in the flour to form a smooth paste, then whisk in the stock, sugar, oregano, basil, and the liquid from the sprouts. Cook on high for 1 minute. Stir in the pimiento and olives, then pour the sauce over the sprouts and sprinkle with the cheese. Microwave on high for 1 minute before serving.

Savoury Pumpkin Flans

THE DELICATE FLAVOUR OF THE PUMPKIN, ENHANCED BY VANILLA,
MAKES THESE FLANS AN IDEAL CHOICE FOR A FIRST COURSE.

Serves 6
Working time: about 20 minutes
Total time: about 40 minutes

Calories **120**
Protein **4g**
Cholesterol **10mg**
Total fat **6g**
Saturated fat **3g**
Sodium **35mg**

1	small pumpkin (about 1 kg/2½ lb), halved horizontally, seeds removed	1
30 g	unsalted butter	1 oz
30 g	flour	1 oz
3 tbsp	evaporated milk	3 tbsp
3	egg whites	3
1 tbsp	brown sugar	1 tbsp
¼ tsp	cinnamon	¼ tsp
¼ tsp	grated nutmeg	¼ tsp
¼ tsp	vanilla extract	¼ tsp
1	lemon, grated rind only	1
2 tbsp	chopped walnuts	2 tbsp

Cut each pumpkin half into four wedges. Place these in a shallow baking dish, cover them with plastic film, pierce the film and microwave them on high for 6 minutes. Rearrange the wedges so that their less-cooked portions face the outside of the dish. Cover the pumpkin once again and microwave on high until the

flesh is tender — 4 to 6 minutes. Let the wedges stand until they are cool enough to handle.

Scoop the pumpkin flesh from the shells and purée it in a food processor. (Alternatively, work the flesh through a food mill or a sieve.) There should be about ½ litre (16 fl oz) of pumpkin purée.

In a bowl, microwave the butter on high for 30 seconds. Stir in the flour to make a smooth paste. Whisk in the evaporated milk and egg whites. Stir this mixture into the purée with the brown sugar, cinnamon, nutmeg, vanilla and lemon rind.

Butter the bottoms of six 17.5 cl (6 fl oz) ramekins. Spoon the pumpkin mixture into the ramekins and arrange them in a circle in the microwave. Cook the pumpkin flans on medium high (70 per cent power) until they start to pull away from the sides of the ramekins — about 10 minutes.

Let the flans stand for 5 minutes before unmoulding them. Loosen a flan by running a knife around the inside of the ramekin. Invert the ramekin on to a plate and rap the bottom of the mould; lift away the mould. Repeat the process to unmould the other flans. Sprinkle the flans with the walnuts before serving.

Turnips on a Bed of Tarragon Apple Sauce

Serves 6
Working time: about 20 minutes
Total time: about 30 minutes

Calories **75**
Protein **1g**
Cholesterol **5mg**
Total fat **2g**
Saturated fat **1g**
Sodium **120mg**

600 g	turnips, peeled and cut into eighths	1 ¼ lb
15 g	unsalted butter	½ oz
2 tbsp	chopped fresh tarragon, or 2 tsp dried tarragon	2 tbsp
250 g	unsweetened apple sauce	8 oz
2 tbsp	dark brown sugar	2 tbsp
⅛ tsp	cinnamon	⅛ tsp
¼ tsp	salt	¼ tsp
	freshly ground black pepper	

Put the butter and chopped tarragon in a round baking dish and microwave them on high for 1 minute. Remove the dish from the oven and stir in the apple sauce, brown sugar, cinnamon, salt and freshly ground pepper. Set the mixture aside.

Place the turnips in one layer in a baking dish and cover them tightly with plastic film. Microwave the turnips on high until they are tender — 8 to 10 minutes. Transfer the turnips to the dish with the apple sauce mixture, arranging them in a circular pattern. Microwave the turnips and apple sauce for 2 minutes on high to heat them through. Let the dish stand for 2 to 3 minutes before serving.

Pickled Okra

Makes 1 litre (1¾ pints) — 16 portions
Working time: about 20 minutes
Total time: about 1 day

Calories **20**
Protein **1g**
Cholesterol **0mg**
Total fat **0g**
Saturated fat **0g**
Sodium **220mg**

250 g	okra left whole if small, or cut into 2 cm (¾ inch) pieces	8 oz
125 g	small cauliflower florets	4 oz
1	carrot, peeled and sliced into 5 mm (¼ inch) rounds	1
1	onion, thinly sliced	1
1	hot green chili pepper, seeded, deribbed and thinly sliced (caution, page 106)	1
2	garlic cloves, slivered	2

Devilled Corn on the Cob

Serves 6
Working time: about 15 minutes
Total time: about 30 minutes

Calories **105**
Protein **3g**
Cholesterol **5mg**
Total fat **4g**
Saturated fat **1g**
Sodium **90mg**

6	ears of sweetcorn, husked	6
½ tsp	celery seeds	½ tsp
½ tsp	dry mustard	½ tsp
1½ tsp	paprika	1½ tsp
¼ tsp	cayenne pepper	¼ tsp
2 tsp	brown sugar	2 tsp
¼ tsp	salt	¼ tsp
1 tbsp	safflower oil	1 tbsp
15 g	unsalted butter	½ oz

In a small bowl, combine the celery seed, mustard, paprika, cayenne, brown sugar and salt. Put the oil and the butter in another small bowl and microwave them on high for 30 seconds to melt the butter. Pour the hot oil and butter into the seasonings, and stir just to mix (overmixing will produce lumps).

Place an ear of sweetcorn on a piece of strong plastic film; brush it well with the seasoning mixture, and wrap it tightly. Repeat the process with the rest of the ears. Pair the ears and arrange them in the microwave so that they form a triangle. Cook on high for 6 minutes. Rearrange the sweetcorn so that the ears on the outside are now on the inside. Microwave on high for 6 minutes more. Let the ears stand for 5 minutes before unwrapping and serving them.

EDITOR'S NOTE: *If the sweetcorn is picked on the day it is to be eaten, reduce the brown sugar in the recipe to 1 teaspoon and apply a slightly thinner coat of the seasoning mixture.*

17.5 cl	distilled white vinegar	6 fl oz
4	bay leaves	4
¼ tsp	cumin seeds	¼ tsp
4	fresh dill sprigs	4
3 tbsp	sugar	3 tbsp
1½ tsp	salt	1½ tsp
12	black peppercorns	12

Place the okra in a bowl with 12.5 cl (4 fl oz) of water. Cover the bowl with plastic film, leaving a corner open, and microwave on high for 3 minutes, stirring once. Drain and set aside.

In a bowl, combine the cauliflower, carrot, onion, chili pepper and garlic with 6 cl (2 fl oz) water. Partially cover the bowl with plastic film and microwave on high for 4 minutes to bring out the colour of the vegetables. Drain the vegetables and refresh them under cold running water. Drain again and combine with the okra. Pack the mixture into two ½ litre (16 fl oz) glass jars, leaving about 1 cm (½ inch) space at the top.

Combine the vinegar, bay leaves, cumin seeds, dill, sugar, salt and peppercorns in a bowl. Microwave on high, stirring after 1 minute, until the vinegar boils — 2 to 3 minutes. Pour the liquid over the vegetables in the jars to immerse them completely, making certain there are two bay leaves and two sprigs of dill in each jar. Cover and refrigerate. Let the flavour mellow for a day or two before serving.

EDITOR'S NOTE: *These pickles must be refrigerated; they will keep for two weeks. They are excellent with grilled meats.*

Pickled Mushrooms

Makes about 750 g (1½ lb) — 10 portions
Working time: about 15 minutes
Total time: about 24 minutes

Calories **9**
Protein **1g**
Cholesterol **0mg**
Total fat **0g**
Saturated fat **0g**
Sodium **45mg**

500 g	open cup or button mushrooms	1 lb
60 cl	distilled malt vinegar	1 pint
2	dried red chili peppers	2
2	blades mace	2
1	bay leaf	1
1	sprig thyme	1
1	small onion, thinly sliced	1
¼ tsp	salt	¼ tsp
6	peppercorns	6

Wipe the mushrooms with kitchen paper to remove any dirt. Open mushrooms may be peeled if preferred. Do not wash the mushrooms.

Put the vinegar and all of the remaining ingredients into a large bowl. Microwave on full power until the vinegar comes to the boil — 7 to 8 minutes. Add the mushrooms and continue to microwave on full power until the mushrooms soften slightly — about 4 minutes — turning the mushrooms in the vinegar after each minute.

Spoon the mushrooms, spices and herbs into a very clean preserving jar, cover completely with the vinegar and seal the jar immediately. Store the pickle in a cool, dry, airy cupboard.

EDITOR'S NOTE: *To ensure that the mushrooms remain completely immersed in the vinegar, place a small ball of waxed paper or plastic film in the top of the jar before sealing.*

Broccoli Steamed with Orange Segments and Caraway

Serves 4
Working time: about 15 minutes
Total time: about 25 minutes

Calories **95**
Protein **6g**
Cholesterol **10mg**
Total fat **4g**
Saturated fat **2g**
Sodium **160mg**

500 g	broccoli, stalks trimmed to within 5 cm (2 inches) of the florets	1 lb
12.5 cl	unsalted chicken or vegetable stock	4 fl oz
1	orange, juice only of one half, other half peeled and divided into segments	1
15 g	unsalted butter	½ oz
1 tbsp	flour	1 tbsp
2 tsp	caraway seeds	2 tsp
¼ tsp	salt	¼ tsp
	freshly ground black pepper	

Peel any broccoli stalk that is more than 1 cm (½ inch) thick and split its base 1 cm (½ inch) deep.

In a small bowl, combine the stock and orange juice. Put the butter in a shallow baking dish and microwave it on high until it is melted — about 30 seconds. Whisk the flour into the butter to form a paste. Pour the stock and orange juice into the flour paste and stir until the mixture is smooth. Microwave the sauce on high for 1½ minutes, stir it, then microwave it on high for another 1½ minutes.

Stir in the orange segments, caraway seeds, salt and pepper. Arrange the broccoli on top of the sauce with the florets towards the centre. Cover the dish with plastic film, leaving one corner open, and microwave it on high for 7 minutes more. Then let the dish stand covered until the broccoli is tender — 3 to 4 minutes.

Transfer the broccoli to a serving dish. Stir the sauce well, then pour it evenly over the broccoli and serve.

Custard Marrows Stuffed with Sweet Potato Purée

Serves 8
Working time: about 15 minutes
Total time: about 35 minutes

Calories **130**
Protein **4g**
Cholesterol **5mg**
Total fat **3g**
Saturated fat **1g**
Sodium **60mg**

8	small custard marrows (about 1 kg/2 lb)	8
350 g	sweet potatoes	12 oz
12.5 cl	plain low-fat yogurt	4 fl oz
30 g	Parmesan cheese, freshly grated	1 oz
	freshly ground black pepper	
⅛ tsp	cinnamon	⅛ tsp
	pinch of ground cloves	
2 tbsp	slivered almonds	2 tbsp

To cook the sweet potatoes, pierce the skin in several places with a skewer or the tip of a knife. Microwave them on high for 6 minutes, turning them over twice during the cooking. Let the sweet potatoes stand for 3 minutes, then peel them and mash them in a bowl. Combine the mashed sweet potatoes with the yogurt, cheese, pepper, cinnamon and cloves, and stir vigorously until smooth.

Cut off the tops of the custard marrows and scoop out the centres with a mellon baller or spoon, leaving a firm shell. Place them cut side down in a baking dish and cover the dish tightly with plastic film. Microwave on high for 4 minutes. Turn the custard marrows over, cover, and microwave on high until tender — 2 to 4 minutes. Stuff the custard marrows with the sweet-potato mixture and sprinkle with the slivered almonds. Microwave them on high for 2 minutes more. Let the dish stand for 2 to 3 minutes before serving.

Kohlrabies and Carrots in a Hot Vinaigrette

Serves 4
Working time: about 15 minutes
Total time: about 20 minutes

Calories **90**
Protein **1g**
Cholesterol **0mg**
Total fat **7g**
Saturated fat **1g**
Sodium **145mg**

2	kohlrabies (about 350 g/12 oz)	2
1	carrot, peeled and sliced into 5 mm (¼ inch) thick rounds	1
2 tsp	white wine vinegar	2 tsp
¼ tsp	salt	¼ tsp
⅛ tsp	white pepper	⅛ tsp
2 tbsp	safflower oil	2 tbsp
1 tsp	honey	1 tsp
1 tbsp	finely cut chives	1 tbsp

Pierce the kohlrabies in several places with a fork. Place them in a dish and cover tightly with plastic film. Microwave the kohlrabies on high for 4 minutes. Turn the kohlrabies over, cover them again, and microwave for 3 minutes more. Remove the dish from the oven and let it stand while you cook the carrot rounds. Place the carrot rounds in a dish and sprinkle them with 1 tablespoon of water. Cover the dish with plastic film, leaving a corner open, and microwave on high for 4 minutes.

Slice off the woody tops of the kohlrabies (about 1 cm/½ inch). Peel the kohlrabies and cut them into 1 cm (½ inch) thick slices. Arrange the kohlrabi slices and carrot rounds in an alternating pattern on a serving plate.

Combine the vinegar, salt and pepper in a glass bowl. Whisk in the oil, honey and 1 tablespoon of water. Microwave the vinaigrette on high for 1 minute, then stir in the chives. Pour the vinaigrette over the vegetables and serve.

EDITOR'S NOTE: *This dish makes an excellent accompaniment for grilled fish.*

Drying Herbs by Microwave

Herbs stand before the microwave oven in which they were dried. From left to right are sage, rosemary, dill, thyme and oregano, each with fresh sprigs nearby.

A cook confronting the enviable dilemma of fresh herbs in overabundance should consider drying the excess for later use. Employing the microwave oven to dry the herbs allows them to be prepared for storage quickly.

Start with fresh herbs from either market or garden; pictured above are five of the best candidates. If you harvest the herbs yourself, cut them in the morning, when the content of aromatic oil in their leaves is highest. Wash the herbs in cool water, pinching off any yellowed or blemished leaves, and spread out the sprigs to dry in the air. Unless their surfaces are completely dry when the herbs go into the microwave oven, the herbs will cook instead of dehydrating.

When the herbs are dry, layer three paper towels on a round glass plate. Arrange a single layer of five or six sprigs of herbs in a circle on the towels and then cover them with another paper towel. The paper traps the water vapour the sprigs release, preventing it from cooking the leaves.

Place the plate in the oven and microwave the herbs on high, rotating the plate and checking the leaves for dryness every 60 seconds. Most herbs require no more than 3 minutes' microwaving. When the herbs feel dry but have not lost their colour, remove the plate and set it aside to cool. Prepare another plate in the same way and microwave a second batch of herbs.

Continue drying herbs in small batches, alternating the plates so that neither one gets too hot to handle. If you are drying more than a dozen batches of herbs, pause for at least 20 minutes at the end of each dozen to let the microwave oven rest. When the dried herbs have cooled, strip the sprigs and put the leaves in airtight jars, or store the sprigs intact for use as garnishes.

Water droplets that appear inside a jar a few hours after it is sealed signal that the contents are not thoroughly dry. If you detect water droplets, empty the jar and wipe it dry, then microwave the herbs for an additional 30 to 60 seconds before returning them to the jar. Store the jars in a cool, dark place.

Jacket Potatoes with Soured Cream, Broccoli and Asparagus

Serves 4
Working time: about 15 minutes
Total time: about 40 minutes

Calories **280**
Protein **8g**
Cholesterol **25mg**
Total fat **9g**
Saturated fat **5g**
Sodium **135mg**

4	large potatoes, scrubbed well, dried, pricked all over with a fork	4
250 g	broccoli	8 oz
125 g	asparagus	4 oz
1 tsp	olive oil	1 tsp
15 cl	soured cream	¼ pint
¼ tsp	salt	¼ tsp
	freshly ground black pepper	
2 tbsp	finely cut chives	2 tbsp
	paprika for garnish	

Peel the broccoli stalks right up to the heads. Cut off the heads and divide them into small florets. Cut the stalks diagonally into thin slices. Thinly peel the asparagus up to the tips. Cut off the tips, then cut the stems into slices.

Put the broccoli and asparagus into a bowl with 2 tablespoons of cold water. Cover with plastic film, leaving a corner open. Microwave on full power until the vegetables are just tender — 2½ to 3 minutes — stirring twice during cooking. Remove and set aside.

Rub the skins of the potatoes with the olive oil. Place on kitchen paper in the microwave. Microwave on high until they are cooked through — about 20 minutes — turning them over half way through cooking.

Put the soured cream into a bowl and season with the salt and pepper. Stir in the chives, broccoli and asparagus. Cut each potato almost in half diagonally, and arrange on a serving dish. Microwave the soured cream mixture for 1 minute, then spoon some into each potato. Sprinkle with paprika and serve.

Creamed Spinach with Shiitake Mushrooms

Serves 4
Working time: about 30 minutes
Total time: about 40 minutes

Calories **75**
Protein **3g**
Cholesterol **15mg**
Total fat **5g**
Saturated fat **3g**
Sodium **185mg**

650 g	spinach, washed, stems removed	1½ lb
25 g	unsalted butter	¾ oz
1 tbsp	flour	1 tbsp
12.5 cl	unsalted chicken or vegetable stock	4 fl oz
60 g	shiitake mushrooms, stems removed, caps wiped clean and thinly sliced	2 oz
6 cl	milk	2 fl oz
⅛ tsp	grated nutmeg	⅛ tsp
¼ tsp	salt	¼ tsp
	freshly ground black pepper	

Put the spinach in a large baking dish and cover it tightly with plastic film. Pierce the film to allow steam to escape. Microwave the spinach on high until it is wilted and tender — about 4 minutes. Transfer it to a colander and pour off any liquid in the dish.

Melt the butter in the baking dish by microwaving it on high for 30 seconds. Whisk the flour into the butter until a smooth paste results, then whisk in the stock. Add the mushrooms to this sauce and cover the dish again with plastic film, pierced as before. Microwave on high until the sauce bubbles — about 2 minutes.

Squeeze the excess moisture from the spinach. Coarsely chop the spinach and add it to the sauce along with the milk, nutmeg, salt and pepper. Mix well to coat the spinach thoroughly with the sauce. Microwave on high for 2 minutes more. Let the dish stand for 2 to 3 minutes before serving.

Leafy Layer

Serves 6
Working time: about 35 minutes
Total time: about 1 hour

Calories **90**
Protein **10g**
Cholesterol **150mg**
Total fat **2g**
Saturated fat **1g**
Sodium **210mg**

6 or 7	large leaves from a green cabbage	6 or 7
250 g	spinach, stems removed	8 oz
250 g	Swiss chard, white stems removed	8 oz
250 g	leeks, trimmed and thinly sliced	8 oz
125 g	sorrel, finely shredded	4 oz
2	eggs	2
1	egg white	1
30 cl	skimmed milk	½ pint
¼ tsp	salt	¼ tsp
	freshly ground black pepper	
1 tbsp	chopped tarragon	1 tbsp
2 tbsp	finely chopped parsley	2 tbsp
2	spring onions, finely chopped	2

To enable the cabbage leaves to be easily moulded, trim away the protruding rib at the back of each leaf until it is level with the rest of the leaf. Wash the cabbage leaves, spinach, chard, leeks and sorrel very thoroughly to remove any grit, keeping each vegetable separate.

Place the cabbage leaves in a large bowl. Cover the bowl with plastic film, leaving one corner open. Microwave on high just long enough to soften the leaves — 3 to 4 minutes. Remove the leaves from the bowl and drain them well on kitchen paper. Repeat this process with the spinach, chard and leeks.

Put the eggs, egg white, milk, salt and pepper into a mixing bowl. Whisk them lightly together, then stir in the herbs and spring onions.

Very lightly butter a deep, round dish, about 20 cm (8 inches) in diameter and 5 cm (2 inches) deep. Neatly line the dish with some of the cabbage leaves, overlapping them to ensure a snug fit and allowing the excess leaf to overhang at the top of the dish.

Fill the lined dish with alternate layers of spinach, chard, leeks, sorrel and herb custard mixture. Place the remaining cabbage leaves on top of the filling, and bring the overhanging leaves in over the top to enclose the filling.

Cover the dish with plastic film, leaving one corner open. Microwave on high until the custard is just set — 18 to 20 minutes. Allow to stand for 5 minutes, then carefully unmould on to a hot serving plate.

EDITOR'S NOTE: *The number of leaves required to line the dish will vary according to the size of the cabbage. If green cabbage and Swiss chard are not available, white cabbage and bok choy or Chinese cabbage may be used instead.*

Vegetable Nutrients

Vegetable, raw, 100 g (3½ oz) unless noted, edible part only

	CALORIES 1900-2900 recommended daily	PROTEIN 47-72 recommended daily	CARBOHYDRATES 230-360 recommended daily	FOLIC ACID 200 recommended daily	VITAMIN A ACTIVITY** 750 recommended daily	VITAMIN C 30 recommended daily	CALCIUM 400-500 recommended daily	SODIUM 2000 maximum daily	POTASSIUM 1,875 minimum daily	DIETARY FIBRE 25-30 recommended daily
		grams	grams	micrograms	micrograms	milligrams	milligrams	milligrams	milligrams	grams
Artichoke, Globe (1 medium)	30	3	11	90	50	15	50	45	43	2
Artichokes, Jerusalem	40	2	15	—	15	4	15	—	—	1
Asparagus	25	3	5	—	270	35	20	2	280	1
Aubergine	15	1	3	20	trace	5	10	3	240	3
Batavian Endive	12	2	1	330	335	12	45	10	380	2
Beans, Green and Wax	25	2	4	20	60	9	21	2	280	3
Beans, Broad	105	8	20	—	65	30	25	4	471	2
Bean Sprouts	35	4	6	30	2	19	7	3	77	3
Beet Greens*	25	2	5	—	1830	30	120	130	570	1
Beetroot	30	1	6	90	trace	6	25	85	300	3
Bok Choy	15	1	1	—	1070	25	165	23	305	trace
Broccoli	25	3	3	130	415	110	100	12	340	4
Brussels Sprouts	25	4	3	110	65	90	100	10	340	4
Cabbage, Chinese	15	2	3	75	45	30	45	25	255	1
Cabbage, Green	20	3	3	90	50	55	55	7	390	3
Cabbage, Red	20	2	3	90	3	55	55	30	300	3
Cabbage, Savoy	25	3	3	90	50	60	75	25	260	3
Carrots	25	1	5	15	2000	6	50	95	220	3
Cauliflower	15	2	2	40	5	60	20	8	350	2
Celeriac	40	2	9	—	0	8	45	100	300	1
Celery	10	1	1	12	trace	7	50	140	280	2
Chicory	10	2	1	50	0	5	15	7	180	—
Collard Greens	10	2	1	140	2790	30	85	10	120	4
Courgettes	20	1	4	50	95	20	30	1	200	1
Cucumbers	10	1	2	16	trace	8	23	13	140	trace
Fennel, Bulb	50	4	10	—	—	—	—	—	—	2
Garlic (1 clove)	4	trace	1	trace	0	1	5	1	12	trace
Kale	55	6	9	—	3000	185	250	75	380	1
Kohlrabi	30	2	6	0	6	66	40	8	370	1
Leeks	30	2	6	30	6	20	60	10	310	3
Lettuce, Cos	10	1	1	34	165	15	25	9	240	2
Mushrooms	15	2	0	25	0	3	3	9	470	3

*contains oxalic acid, which may inhibit absorption of the vegetable's calcium   **measured in retinol equivalents   A dash indicates that no information was available.

Vegetable, raw, 100 g (3½ oz) unless noted, edible part only

	CALORIES 1900-2900 recommended daily	PROTEIN 47-72 recommended daily	CARBOHYDRATES 230-360 recommended daily	FOLIC ACID 200 recommended daily	VITAMIN A ACTIVITY** 750 recommended daily	VITAMIN C 30 recommended daily	CALCIUM 400-500 recommended daily	SODIUM 2000 maximum daily	POTASSIUM 1,875 minimum daily	DIETARY FIBRE 25-30 recommended daily
		grams	grams	micrograms	micrograms	milligrams	milligrams	milligrams	milligrams	grams
Mustard Greens	30	3	6	—	2100	95	185	32	377	1
Okra	20	2	2	100	15	25	70	7	190	3
Onions	25	1	5	15	0	10	30	10	140	1
Parsley (5 tbsp chopped)	5	1	trace	—	1165	40	85	8	270	2
Parsnips	50	2	11	65	0	15	55	17	340	4
Peas, Green (shelled)	65	6	10	—	50	25	15	1	340	5
Peas, Mange-Tout and Sugar Snap	50	3	12	—	65	50	60	6	170	4
Peppers, Chili (red)	116	6	10	—	1100	95	85	25	1285	—
(green)	20	1	5	—	250	130	9	13	215	1
Peppers, Sweet	15	1	2	11	90	100	9	2	210	1
Potatoes	90	2	20	15	trace	15	8	7	570	2
Pumpkin	15	1	4	13	250	5	40	1	310	1
Radishes	15	1	3	24	trace	25	45	60	240	1
Salsify	50	3	18	—	0	11	60	10	380	2
Shallots (1 tbsp chopped)	7	trace	2	—	—	1	4	1	33	trace
Spinach* (raw)	25	3	4	—	2430	30	95	70	470	1
(cooked)	30	5	1	140	2000	25	600	120	490	6
Spring Onions (green part included)	35	1	9	40	600	10	140	13	230	3
Squash, Butternut	55	1	14	—	1710	9	30	1	485	1
Squash, Chayote	30	1	7	—	6	20	13	5	102	1
Squash, Custard Marrow	20	1	4	—	125	20	30	1	202	1
Squash, Spaghetti	10	trace	2	4	4	1	6	5	30	1
Squash, Yellow	20	1	8	25	45	25	30	1	200	1
Swedes	20	1	4	27	0	25	55	50	140	3
Sweet Potatoes	90	1	20	50	665	25	20	20	320	3
Sweetcorn	125	4	25	50	40	9	4	1	300	4
Swiss Chard*	25	2	5	—	1950	30	90	145	550	1
Tomatoes	14	1	3	30	100	20	13	3	290	2
Turnips	20	1	4	20	0	25	60	60	240	3
Vine Leaves (each)	15	4	trace	—	385	15	390	—	45	5
Water Chestnuts	50	1	13	—	0	6	20	14	155	—
Watercress	14	3	1	200	500	60	220	60	310	4

The figures given here should be taken as a guide only: the composition of vegetables can vary

Shopping and Storage

Vegetable	Look for:	Avoid:	How to store:
Artichokes, globe	Heavy, blemish-free, bright green globes with closed leaves. In winter, globes may be marked by small, uniform brown streaks caused by frost.	Bruised globes; globes with curling leaves; lightweight, dried-out or pale globes.	Refrigerate in a tightly covered container or closed plastic bag to retain moisture. Will keep up to two weeks.
Artichokes, Jerusalem	Firm, pale brown tubers with smooth, unwrinkled skin (may be tinged with yellow, purple or pink); specimens that are heavy for their size.	Soft tubers with wrinkled or broken skin; lightweight or mouldy tubers.	Refrigerate unwrapped. Will keep for up to one week.
Asparagus	Firm, bright green spears with closed, compact tips.	Dried-out spears with open tips; curved, soft spears with discoloured tips.	Stand upright in a container filled with 2.5 to 5 cm (1 to 2 inches) of water and cover loosely, or wrap stem ends in damp paper towels and enclose bundles in plastic film. Do not wash; moisture produces mould on tips. Will keep for a few days.
Aubergine	Small to medium specimens, heavy in relation to size; smooth, glossy, purplish black skin that springs back when pressed.	Large, lightweight specimens; dull, shrivelled or brown-spotted skin; soft (over-ripe) or hard (under-ripe) skins.	Refrigerate unwrapped or in a paper bag. Will keep for three to four days.
Batavian endive	Tightly packed heads with crisp green leaves.	Loose heads with wilted, bruised or yellowing leaves.	Use as soon as possible. Will keep refrigerated in a plastic bag for a few days.
Bean sprouts	Short, crisp, pale yellow-white sprouts.	Long, limp sprouts; tinges of brown or mould.	Best when used immediately, but will keep for a day or two refrigerated in a tightly closed plastic bag.
Beans, broad	Plump, moist, firm pods.	Withered or blemished pods; brown spots.	Refrigerate in a plastic bag for not more than a few days.
Beans, French	Crisp, slender, thin-walled pods with smooth skin.	Dull, discoloured or flabby pods; large, thick-walled pods; wrinkled skin.	Refrigerate in a plastic bag for not more than a few days.
Beans, wax	Vivid yellow, slender, thin-walled pods with smooth skin.	Dull, flabby pods streaked or spotted brown; thick-walled pods; wrinkled skin.	Refrigerate in a plastic bag for not more than a few days.
Beet greens	Tender, thin-ribbed, fresh and clean leaves.	Wilted or decayed leaves.	Use as soon as possible; if necessary, refrigerate in a plastic bag for one or two days.
Beetroots	Small to medium, smooth, round, deep red specimens. Leafy tops should be green to red-green and crisp. If tops have been removed, 2.5 to 5 cm (1 to 2 inches) of stem should remain lest colour bleed out.	Large beets (they may be tough); spotted, scaly or bruised skin; wilted tops.	Cut off tops immediately, leaving 2.5 to 5 cm (1 to 2 inches) of stem attached. Keep roots intact. Refrigerate in a plastic bag for up to two weeks.
Bok choy	Straight, firm white stalks with crisp, shiny green or greenish white leaves.	Limp stalks with wilted leaves.	Refrigerate in a plastic bag. Will keep for a few days.
Broccoli	Tightly closed heads of broccoli that have dark green or purplish buds; firm stems with fresh leaves.	Open buds with yellow flowers; flabby stems with wilted leaves.	Refrigerate in a perforated plastic bag. Will keep for a week or more.
Brussels sprouts	Small, firm, bright green heads with fresh outer leaves.	Pale heads with loose, wilted or curling outer leaves; heads with holes (evidence of insect infestation).	Use as soon as possible. If necessary, refrigerate in a plastic bag for a day or two.
Cabbage, Chinese	Firm, smooth white stems with crisp green, greenish white or pale yellow leaves.	Flabby stems; wilted leaves.	Refrigerate in a plastic bag. Will keep for a few days.

Vegetable	Look for:	Avoid:	How to store:
Cabbage, green	Light-green heads that are heavy in relation to size.	White heads (over-mature); lightweight heads; yellowing or discoloured leaves.	Refrigerate in a plastic bag for up to 10 days.
Cabbage, red	Bright red or purplish heads that are heavy in relation to size; intact, unblemished outer leaves.	Large, lightweight heads; blemished outer leaves or heads with outer leaves trimmed.	Refrigerate in a plastic bag for up to 10 days.
Cabbage, Savoy	Firm heads that are heavy in relation to size; crinkly, intact, green outer leaves.	Lightweight heads; yellow, wilted or blemished outer leaves.	Refrigerate in a plastic bag. Will keep for a week or more.
Carrots	Firm, smooth, bright orange specimens with fresh green tops, if any.	Flabby, cracked or shrivelled carrots; pale orange colour; green-tinged tips; hairy roots; wilted tops.	Cut off green tops immediately. Refrigerate carrots in a plastic bag for two weeks or more.
Cauliflower	Compact heads, or curds, with white to creamy white florets. Fresh green leaves.	Spread-out florets; bruised or brown-spotted curd; yellow leaves.	Refrigerate in a plastic bag. Will keep for several days.
Celeriac	Small, firm knobs less than 10 cm (4 inches) in diameter.	Large knobs (they may be woody); knobs with soft spots; cracked knobs; wilted roots.	Trim tops and roots. Refrigerate celeriac in a plastic bag for up to one week.
Celery	Tightly closed bunch; light-green stalks; fresh, green leaves.	Loosely formed bunch; flabby or blemished stalks; wilted or yellow leaves.	Refrigerate in a plastic bag. Will keep for one to two weeks.
Chicory	Crisp, firm, compact heads; creamy white stalks with pale yellow tips.	Loose heads; heads with brown spots or streaks.	Refrigerate in a paper bag. Will keep for several days.
Courgettes	Small to medium-sized, firm, smooth, plump specimens; shiny, dark green skin. There is also a yellow variety.	Specimens more than 20 cm (8 inches) long; dull skin; blemished skin; soft or flabby flesh; wrinkled ends.	Refrigerate unwrapped. Will keep for up to four days.
Cucumbers	Firm flesh; uniformly dark-green skin; medium size.	Large specimens with yellow or brown areas on skin; shrivelled ends; soft flesh.	Refrigerate unwrapped or in a paper bag. Will keep for a few days.
Fennel, bulb	Firm, white bulbs; straight stalks; fresh, green, feathery leaves.	Brown-spotted bulbs; spongy stalks; wilted leaves.	Refrigerate in a plastic bag. Will keep for a few days.
Garlic	Firm bulbs with unbroken skin; bulbs that are heavy for their size; purple or white skin, depending on the variety.	Bulbs with dried-out, shrivelled cloves; soft or sprouted bulbs; bulbs with broken skins.	Store in a cool, dry, well-ventilated area. Keep away from other foods and direct light. Will keep well for four to six weeks.
Kale	Crisp, curled leaves that are dark green, silver-green or blue-green.	Soft leaves; yellowed or blemished leaves.	Use as soon as possible. May be refrigerated in a plastic bag for a few days.
Kohlrabi	Small heads, about 5 cm (2 inches) in diameter or smaller; thin, tender, unblemished skin.	Large heads (they can be tough); cracked heads; tough skins.	Refrigerate unwrapped. Will keep for several days.
Leeks	Young bulbs no more than 4 cm (1½ inches) in diameter; smooth bulbs with firmly attached roots and no discoloration; bright green, firm, tightly closed tops.	Large bulbs (they may be tough); bruised, discoloured or slimy bulbs; open, flabby, wilted or yellowish leaves.	Refrigerate in a plastic bag. Will keep for a week or more.
Lettuce, cos	Compact heads with crisp, dark green leaves.	Wilted leaves; leaves, with brown spots or black edges; bruised, broken or brown-streaked stems.	Refrigerate in a plastic bag. Will keep for a few days.
Mushrooms	White, cream or brown, even-coloured, smooth-skinned caps.	Shrivelled caps; slimy or soft caps.	Refrigerate in an open paper bag or on a tray covered with a damp paper towel. Do not store in a plastic bag — mushrooms need air circulation. Will keep for a few days.

Vegetable	Look for:	Avoid:	How to store:
Mustard greens	Small, fresh leaves that are light to dark green; bronze tint on leaves is acceptable.	Large, yellowing or wilted leaves; leaves with seed stems.	Refrigerate for two or three days.
Okra	Small, bright green, crisp pods, about 5 to 10 cm (2 to 4 inches) long with flexible tips.	Large pods (they may be tough and fibrous); dull colour; hard skin or tips; shrivelled or black-spotted skin.	Refrigerate unwrapped or in a paper bag. Will keep for up to two days.
Onions	Firm flesh with dry, papery outer skin, heavy in relation to size.	Soft, spongy flesh; thick stem end with green sprouts; mouldy or blemished skin.	Store in a cool, dark, dry, well-ventilated area. Will keep for about four weeks.
Parsley	Crisp, bright green bunches; leaves springy to the touch.	Flabby stems and wilted leaves; yellow leaves or black-edged leaves.	Untie bunch, trim stems, and stand bunch upright in 2.5 cm (1 inch) of water. Cover with plastic film and refrigerate. Will keep for one to two weeks.
Parsnips	Small to medium specimens; plump and firm with smooth skin and fresh green tops if attached.	Large, soft, cracked or shrivelled specimens; dry, dull or spotted skin; wilted tops.	Cut off the tops and refrigerate the parsnips in a plastic bag. Will keep for up to 10 days.
Peas, green	Shiny, bright green, crisp pods about 5 to 10 cm (3 to 4 inches) long and well filled out.	Yellowing, spotted or scaly pods; soft, wilted or swollen pods; pods with a dull green colour.	Use immediately. Will keep for a day or two refrigerated in a paper bag.
Peas, mange-tout	Flat, shiny, crisp pods with a bright green colour.	Yellowish or dull green pods; soft, shrivelled or wilted pods.	Use immediately. Will keep for a few days refrigerated in a paper bag.
Peas, sugar snap	Small, shiny, bright green pods with a crisp texture.	Yellowish or dull green pods; soft, shrivelled or wilted pods.	Use immediately. Will keep for a few days refrigerated in a paper bag.
Peppers, chili	Plump, glossy, crisp chilies. (Green chilies often are hotter than red but will redden during storage and mellow in flavour.)	Shrivelled, lustreless chilies; any with dark spots.	Refrigerate unwrapped or in a paper bag. Will keep for up to two weeks.
Peppers, sweet	Shiny, firm, thick-skinned peppers, either green, red or yellow. (Red and yellow peppers are sweet, ripened forms of green pepper; for flavour, the red and yellow varieties are interchangeable.)	Soft flesh; thin or wrinkled skin; dull-coloured or brown-spotted skin.	Refrigerate unwrapped or in a paper bag. Will keep for several days. Do not store in a plastic bag.
Potatoes (baking)	Smooth, firm, dull-skinned specimens that are relatively clean.	Sprouting eyes; potatoes with deep cracks or soft spots; shrivelled skin.	Store in a cool, dark, dry, well-ventilated area. Do not refrigerate. Will keep for a month or more.
Potatoes (boiling)	Smooth, firm, shiny-skinned specimens.	Cut, bruised or green-tinged specimens.	Store in a cool — ideal temperature is 4° to 10°C (45° to 50°F) — dark area with good ventilation. Do not refrigerate. Will keep for a month or more if stored properly, a week or two at normal room temperature.
Pumpkin	Firm rind with no spots or cracks.	Large pumpkins; soft, cracked or spotted skin.	Store in a cool, dark, dry place. Will keep for two to three months if stored between 10° and 13°C (50° and 55°F).
Radishes	Firm flesh; smooth unblemished skin; fresh green leaves, if any.	Spongy flesh; dry, cracked or black-spotted skin; wilted or yellowing leaves, if any.	Remove the tops. Refrigerate in a perforated plastic bag. Will keep for two to three weeks.
Salsify and Scorzonera	Medium-sized, firm-fleshed, clean specimens.	Large specimens (they may taste woody); soft flesh; shrivelled skin.	Refrigerate unwrapped. Will keep for a few days.
Shallots	Firm, plump, dry bulbs with skin intact.	Spongy and shrivelled bulbs; bulbs that have sprouted.	Store in a cool, dry, well-ventilated place for up to two months.
Sorrel	Young, tender green leaves.	Tough, leathery, overgrown or discoloured leaves.	Use as soon as possible. Can be refrigerated in a plastic bag for a day or two.

Vegetable	Look for:	Avoid:	How to store:
Spinach	Crisp, dark green, shiny leaves, flat or crinkly. Minimal amount of stems.	Wilted, bruised, blackened or yellowed leaves.	Use as soon as possible. Can be refrigerated in a plastic bag for a day or two.
Spring greens	Crisp, pale green leaves; tender, young stems.	Wilted, blemished or yellowing leaves; coarse, fibrous stems.	Use as soon as possible. May be refrigerated in a plastic bag for two days.
Spring onions	Solid white bulbs with root hairs firmly attached. Straight, crisp, bright green tops.	Discoloured or slimy skin on bulbs; flabby root hairs; soft or damaged leaves.	Refrigerate unwrapped or in a paper bag. Will keep for a few days.
Squash, butternut	Cylindrical specimens 25 to 28 cm (10 to 11 inches) long with smooth, uniformly tan skin; heavy in relation to size.	Green-tinted skin; specimens with soft spots; lightweight specimens.	Store in a cool, dark, dry place with good ventilation for one to two months. Do not refrigerate.
Squash, chayote	Lime green specimens with firm flesh.	Soft or spongy flesh; pale green colour.	Refrigerate unwrapped. Will keep for two to three months.
Squash, custard marrow	Flat, scalloped specimens less than 10 cm (4 inches) in diameter; pale green, white or greenish yellow colour; smooth, shiny skin; heavy in relation to size.	Specimens more than 10 cm (4 inches) in diameter; dull, shrivelled, cut, bruised or blemished skin.	Refrigerate unwrapped. Will keep for several days.
Squash, spaghetti	Oval, creamy white or pale yellow specimens 23 to 30 cm (9 to 12 inches) long; hard skin; heavy in relation to size.	Lightweight or cracked specimens; soft or spotted patches on skin.	Will keep at room temperature for one week; in a cool, dry, dark area with good ventilation for one to two months.
Squash, yellow	Small to medium-sized, firm specimens; smooth or slightly pebbled skin; shiny, pale yellow colour; can have straight or crooked neck.	Specimens more than 20 cm (8 inches) long; bright yellow, heavily pebbled skin; blemished, cut or dull skin; flabby flesh.	Refrigerate unwrapped. Will keep for three to four days.
Swedes	Firm flesh; heavy in relation to size; smooth skin.	Lightweight specimens; cracked, cut or blemished skin.	Refrigerate in a plastic bag. Will keep for two to three weeks.
Sweet potatoes	Firm, medium-sized specimens with tapered ends and smooth, unbroken, dry skin.	Specimens with bruised or blemished flesh (soft spots mean the sweet potato will deteriorate rapidly).	Keep in a cool, dry, dark area with good ventilation. Do not refrigerate. Can be stored for several weeks.
Sweetcorn	Green, cool-feeling husks with silky yellow tassels. Pull back husk to check for plump, pale, tightly arranged kernels.	Dried-out or yellow husks; brown decay at tassel end; immature kernels at tip of cob; oversized, dark-coloured kernels; loosely spaced kernels.	Use as soon as possible. Refrigerate in a paper bag immediately after purchase. Remove husks just before cooking. Will keep refrigerated for a day or two.
Swiss chard	Firm, white or reddish stalks; fresh green, yellowish or reddish leaves.	Flabby stalks; faded, wilted or blemished leaves.	Refrigerate in a plastic bag. The trimmed leaves will keep for only a few days; the separated stalks will keep for as long as 10 days.
Tomatoes	Firm, plump, red specimens; heavy in relation to size.	Soft, bruised specimens; cracks or yellowing at stem end; mouldy or broken skin.	If unripe, ripen at room temperature in a paper bag or a bowl. Keep away from direct sunlight. Refrigerate tomatoes only when they are fully ripe.
Turnips	Small to medium-sized specimens; smooth skin and firm flesh; minimum of roots; crisp green tops, if attached.	Large specimens with many roots; blemished, yellowed or wilted tops.	Remove tops and store in a cool, dry, well-ventilated place for a few days. Or refrigerate in a plastic bag for up to one week.
Vine leaves	Fresh, light-green leaves.	Dark green leaves with white spots.	Refrigerate in acidulated water for up to two weeks. Discard if mould appears.
Water chestnuts	Firm, plump specimens at least 2.5 cm (1 inch) in diameter, with dark brown skins.	Small specimens; dry, shrivelled skin.	Refrigerate unpeeled. Will keep for up to one week.
Watercress	Bunches with crisp stems and bright green, fresh leaves.	Bunches with flabby stems and wilted or yellowing leaves.	Untie stems and trim off their bases. Stand the bunch upright in a container filled with 2.5 cm (1 inch) of water, cover with plastic film and refrigerate. Will keep for about one week.

A Dictionary of Cuts

Knowing how to cut vegetables into various shapes adds variety to cooking. Larger cuts — dice or cubes, julienne and slices — allow a vegetable to retain its characteristic texture. Smaller cuts, among them the very fine chopping of garlic cloves, help to release the vegetable's flavour throughout the cooking. The photographs below demonstrate the seven cuts that are most commonly called for in *Fresh Ways with Vegetables*.

THINLY SLICED CARROT

DIAGONALLY SLICED CARROT

DICED SWEET RED PEPPER

JULIENNED CARROT

VERY FINELY CHOPPED GARLIC

FINELY CHOPPED ONION

COARSELY CHOPPED ONION

Chicken Stock

Makes 2 to 3 litres (3½ to 5 pints)
Working time: about 20 minutes
Total time: about 3 hours

2 to 2.5 kg	uncooked chicken trimmings and bones (preferably wings, necks and backs), the bones cracked with a heavy knife	4 to 5 lb
2	carrots, scrubbed, sliced into 1 cm (½ inch) rounds	2
3	sticks celery, sliced into 2.5 cm (1 inch) lengths	3
2	large onions, cut in half, one half stuck with 2 cloves	2
2	fresh thyme sprigs, or ½ tsp dried thyme	2
1 or 2	bay leaves	1 or 2
10 to 15	parsley stems	10 to 15
5	black peppercorns	5

Put the trimmings and bones in a heavy stock-pot and pour in enough water to cover them by 5 cm (2 inches). Slowly bring the liquid to the boil, skimming off the scum that rises to the surface. Boil for 10 minutes, skimming and adding a little cold water from time to time to help precipitate the scum.

Add the vegetables, herbs and peppercorns, and submerge them in the liquid. If necessary, add enough additional water to cover the vegetables and bones. Reduce the heat to low. Simmer the mixture for 2 to 3 hours, skimming once more during the process.

Strain the stock and allow it to stand until tepid, then refrigerate it overnight or freeze it long enough for the fat to congeal. Spoon off and discard the layer of fat.

Tightly covered and refrigerated, the stock may safely be kept for three to four days. Stored in small, tightly covered freezer containers and frozen, the stock may be kept for as long as six months.

EDITOR'S NOTE: *The chicken gizzard and heart, along with the bird's uncooked skin, may be used to prepare the stock. Wings and necks — rich in natural gelatine — produce a particularly gelatinous stock, ideal for sauces and jellied dishes.*

Because the recipes in this book contain little salt, cooks may wish to prepare a stock with a more complex flavour. Unpeeled, lightly crushed garlic cloves, dried basil, additional bay leaves or parsley stems — even a sweet potato cut in half — may be used to heighten the flavour of the stock without overwhelming it.

Vegetable Stock

Makes about 1½ litres (2½ pints)
Working time: about 25 minutes
Total time: about 1 hour and 30 minutes

3	sticks celery with leaves, finely chopped	3
3	carrots, scrubbed, sliced into 3 mm (⅛ inch) rounds	3
3	large onions (about 750 g/1½ lb), coarsely chopped	3
2	large broccoli stems, coarsely chopped (optional)	2
1	medium turnip, peeled and cut into 1 cm (½ inch) cubes	1
5	garlic cloves, coarsely chopped	5
25 g	parsley (with stems), coarsely chopped	¾ oz
10	black peppercorns	10
2	fresh thyme sprigs, or 1 tsp dried thyme	2
2	bay leaves	2

Put the celery, carrots, onions, broccoli if you are using it, turnip, garlic, parsley and peppercorns in a heavy stock-pot. Pour in enough water to cover them by 5 cm (2 inches). Slowly bring the liquid to the boil over medium heat, skimming off any scum that rises to the surface. When the liquid reaches the boil, add the thyme and bay leaves. Stir the stock once and reduce the heat to low; cover the pot, leaving the lid slightly ajar. Let the stock simmer undisturbed for 1 hour.

Strain the stock into a large bowl, pressing down lightly on the vegetables to extract all their liquid. Discard the vegetables. Allow the stock to stand until it is tepid, then refrigerate or freeze it.

Tightly covered and refrigerated, the stock may safely be kept for five to six days. Stored in small, tightly covered freezer containers and frozen, the stock may be kept for as long as six months.

Glossary

Acidulated water: a dilute solution of lemon juice in water, used to keep certain vegetables from discolouring after they are peeled.

Balsamic vinegar: a mild, extremely fragrant wine-based vinegar made in northern Italy. Traditionally, the vinegar is aged for at least seven years in a series of casks made of various woods.

Basil: a leafy herb with a strong, spicy aroma when fresh, often used in Italian cooking. Covered with olive oil and refrigerated in a tightly sealed container, fresh basil leaves may be kept for several months.

Bay leaves: the aromatic leaves of *Laurus nobilis* — a Mediterranean evergreen — used fresh or dried to flavour stocks and stews; also available in powder form. Dried bay leaves when broken have very sharp edges and can injure internally, so they should be removed before serving.

Beet greens: the tops of beetroot, sometimes sold separately, eaten as a nutritious green vegetable. Certain varieties are grown as much for their tops as for their roots.

Blanc: a cooking liquid made by adding flour and lemon juice to water in order to keep certain vegetables from discolouring as they cook.

Blanch: to partially cook food by briefly immersing it in boiling water. Blanching makes thin-skinned fruits and vegetables easier to peel; it can also mellow strong flavours. See also Parboil.

Bok choy (also called Chinese chard): a sweet-tasting cruciferous vegetable that grows in a celery-like bunch, with smooth white stalks and wide, dark-green leaves.

Bouquet garni: several herbs — the classic three are parsley, thyme and bay leaf — tied together or wrapped in muslin and used to flavour a stock, sauce, braise or stew. The bouquet garni is removed and discarded at the end of the cooking time.

Braise: to cook meat, vegetables or a combination of the two with some liquid over low heat. Braising can be done in the oven or on top of the stove. It helps to moisten and tenderize the food.

Bulb fennel: see Fennel.

Burghul (also called bulgur): a type of cracked wheat, where the kernels are steamed and dried before being crushed.

Buttermilk: a tangy, low-fat, cultured milk product whose slight acidity makes it an ideal marinade base for poultry.

Calorie (or kilocalorie): a precise measure of the energy food supplies when it is broken down for use in the body.

Caramelize: to heat sugar or a food naturally rich in sugar, such as garlic or onion, until the sugar turns brown and syrupy.

Cardamom: the bittersweet, aromatic dried seeds or whole pods of a plant in the ginger family. Often used in curries.

Cayenne pepper: a fiery powder ground from the seeds and pods of red peppers. Used in small amounts to heighten other flavours.

Celeriac (also called celery root): the knobby, tuberous root of a plant in the celery family.

Chayote (also called christophine): a pear-shaped, deeply furrowed, soft-skinned squash originally grown in Central America. Its skin is pale green, its flesh pale green to white; its skin, flesh and seed are all edible.

Chicory: a small, cigar-shaped vegetable, composed of many tightly wrapped white to pale-yellow leaves. Can be cooked, or eaten raw in salads.

Chili peppers: hot or mild red, yellow or green members of the pepper family. Fresh or dried, most chili peppers contain volatile oils that can irritate the skin and eyes; they must be handled with extreme care *(caution, page 106)*.

Chinese cabbage (also called Chinese leaves): an elongated cabbage resembling cos lettuce, with long broad ribs and crinkled, light green to white leaves.

Chinese chard: see Bok choy.

Cholesterol: a wax-like substance manufactured in the human body and also found in foods of animal origin. Although a certain amount of cholesterol is necessary for proper body functioning, an excess can accumulate in the arteries, contributing to heart disease. See also Monounsaturated fats; Polyunsaturated fats; Saturated fats.

Coriander (also called cilantro): the pungent, peppery leaves of the coriander plant or its earthy tasting dried seeds. It is a common seasoning in Middle-Eastern, Oriental and Latin-American cookery.

Couscous: cereal processed from semolina into pellets, traditionally steamed and served with meat and vegetables in the classic North African stew of the same name.

Cruciferous vegetables: certain members of the mustard, cabbage and turnip families with cross-shaped flowers and strong aromas and flavours. The genus includes bok choy, broccoli, Brussels sprouts, cabbage, cauliflower, horseradish, kohlrabi, mustard greens, radishes, swedes, turnips and watercress.

Cumin: the aromatic seeds of an umbelliferous plant similar to fennel used, whole or powdered, as a spice, especially in Indian and Latin-American dishes. Toasting gives it a nutty flavour.

Daikon radish (also called mooli): a long, white Japanese radish.

Dark sesame oil (also called Oriental sesame oil): a dark, polyunsaturated oil with a relatively low burning point, most often used as a seasoning; it should not be confused or replaced with lighter sesame oils.

Dietary fibre: a plant-cell material that is undigested or only partially digested in the human body, but which promotes healthy digestion of other food matter.

Dijon mustard: a smooth or grainy hot mustard once manufactured only in Dijon, France; may be flavoured with herbs, green peppercorns or white wine.

Fennel: a herb (also called wild fennel) whose feathery leaves and dried seeds have a mild anise flavour and are much used for flavouring. Its vegetable relative, the bulb — or Florence — fennel (also called finocchio) can be cooked, or eaten raw in salads.

Fermented black beans: soya beans that have been cured in salt, sometimes with citrus peel; used in Chinese dishes. To remove their excess salt, rinse the beans before use.

Fibre: see Dietary fibre.

Ginger: the spicy, buff-coloured root of the ginger plant, used as a seasoning either fresh, or dried in powder form.

Gratin: a baked dish with a crunchy topping of breadcrumbs or grated cheese browned in the oven or under the grill.

Jerusalem artichoke: neither an artichoke nor from Jerusalem, this vegetable is the tuberous root of a member of the sunflower family. In texture, colour and flavour, it resembles the water chestnut. "Jerusalem" may derive from the Italian word "girasole", meaning a plant whose flowers turn towards the sun.

Julienne: the French term for vegetables or other food cut into strips.

Juniper berries: the berries of the juniper tree, used as the key flavouring in gin as well as in pork dishes and sauerkraut. Whole berries should be removed from a dish before it is served.

Kohlrabi: a cruciferous vegetable whose major edible part is an enlarged part of the stem, a light-green or lavender bulb.

Mace: the ground aril, or covering, that encases the nutmeg seed.

Mange-tout: flat green pea pods eaten whole, with only stems and strings removed.

Marjoram: sweet marjoram and its heartier relative pot marjoram are aromatic herbs related to oregano, but milder in flavour.

Monounsaturated fats: one of the three types of fats found in foods. Monounsaturated fats are believed not to raise the level of cholesterol in the blood.

Mozzarella: soft kneaded cheese from southern Italy, traditionally made from buffalo's milk, but now also made from cow's milk. Full-fat mozzarella has a fat content of 40 to 50 per cent, but lower-fat versions are available. The low-fat mozzarella used in the recipes in this book has a fat content of only about 16 per cent.

Non-reactive pan: a cooking vessel whose surface does not chemically react with food. Materials used include stainless steel, enamel, glass and some alloys. Untreated cast iron and aluminium may react with acids, producing discoloration or a peculiar taste.

Olive oil: any of various grades of oil extracted from olives. Extra virgin olive oil has a full, fruity flavour and the lowest acidity. Virgin olive is slightly higher in acidity and lighter in flavour. Pure olive oil, a processed blend of olive oils, has the highest acidity and the lightest taste.

Paprika: a slightly sweet, spicy, bright-red powder produced by grinding dried red peppers. The best type of paprika is Hungarian.

Parboil: to partially cook a food in liquid in order to prepare it for a second cooking method — for example, brief heating in a sauce — that would otherwise leave it underdone.

Phyllo (also spelt "filo"): a paper-thin flour-and-water pastry popular in Greece and the Middle East. It can be made at home or bought, fresh or frozen, from delicatessens and shops specializing in Middle-Eastern food.

Pine-nuts: seeds from the cones of the stone pine, a tree native to the Mediterranean. Pine-nuts are used in pesto and other sauces; their buttery flavour can be brought out by light toasting.

Polyunsaturated fats: one of the three types of fats found in foods. They exist in abundance in such vegetable oils as safflower, sunflower, corn and soya bean. Polyunsaturated fats lower the level of cholesterol in the blood.

Purée: to reduce food to a smooth, even, pulp-like consistency by mashing it, passing it through a sieve, or processing it in a blender or food processor.

Puréed tomatoes: purée made from skinned fresh or canned tomatoes. Available commercially, but should not be confused with the thicker, concentrated tomato paste sometimes labelled tomato purée.

Ramekin: a small, round, straight-sided glass or porcelain mould, used to bake a single serving of food.

Recommended Daily Amount (RDA): the average daily amount of an essential nutrient recommended for healthy people by the U.K. Department of Health and Social Security.

Reduce: to boil down a liquid in order to concentrate its flavour or thicken its consistency.

Ricotta: soft, mild, white Italian cheese, made from cow's or sheep's milk. Full-fat ricotta has a fat content of 20 to 30 per cent, but the low-fat ricotta used in the recipes in this book has a fat content of only about 8 per cent.

Rocket (also called arugula): a peppery-flavoured salad plant with long, leafy stems, popular in Italy.

Rice vinegar: a mild, fragrant vinegar that is less sweet than cider vinegar and not as harsh as distilled malt vinegar. Japanese rice vinegar is milder than the Chinese variety.

Safflower oil: a vegetable oil that contains the highest proportion of polyunsaturated fats.

Saffron: the dried, yellowish-red stigmas (or threads) of the saffron crocus, which yield a powerful yellow colour as well as a pungent flavour. Powdered saffron may be substituted for the threads but has less flavour.

Salsify: a slender, tapering root, about twice the length of a carrot, with a white or yellowish skin and a faint oysterish flavour. See also Scorzonera.

Saturated fats: one of the three types of fat found in foods. They exist in abundance in animal products and coconut and palm oils; they raise the level of cholesterol in the blood. Because high blood-cholesterol levels may cause heart disease, saturated fat consumption should be restricted to less than 15 per cent of the calories provided by the daily diet.

Sauté: to cook a food quickly in a small amount of hot fat, usually in an uncovered frying pan.

Savoy cabbage: a variety of round cabbage with a mild flavour and crisp, crinkly leaves.

Scorzonera: a thin, long cylindrical root with brown or blackish skin, very similar in shape and taste to salsify (see above).

Sesame oil: see Dark sesame oil.

Sesame paste: see Tahini.

Shallot: a mild variety of the onion, with a subtle flavour and papery, red-brown skin.

Shiitake mushroom: a strongly flavoured mushroom originally cultivated in Japan. It is sold fresh or dried; the dried version should be stored in a cool, dry place and may be reconstituted by soaking in warm water.

Sichuan pepper (also called Chinese pepper, Japanese pepper or anise pepper): a dried shrub berry with a tart, aromatic flavour that is less piquant than black pepper.

Simmer: to cook a liquid or sauce just below its boiling point so that the liquid's surface barely ripples.

Sodium: a nutrient essential to maintaining the proper balance of fluids in the body. In most diets, a major source of the element is table salt, made up of 40 per cent sodium. Excess sodium may contribute to high blood pressure, which increases the risk of heart disease. One teaspoon (5.5 g) of salt, with 2,132 milligrams of sodium, contains just over the maximum daily amount recommended by the World Health Organization.

Sorrel: a green-leafed herb with a fresh, acid taste, used for flavouring, and in soups and sauces. It has a delicate leaf structure that breaks down to a purée on contact with heat.

Soy sauce: a savoury, salty brown liquid made from fermented soya beans and available in both light and dark versions. One tablespoon of ordinary soy sauce contains 1,030 milligrams of sodium; lower-sodium variations, as used in the recipes in this book, may contain half that amount.

Spaghetti squash: a yellow-skinned squash whose cooked flesh resembles strands of spaghetti.

Steam: to cook food in the vapour from boiling water; steaming is one of the best cooking techniques for preserving vegetables' nutrients and flavours.

Stir-fry: to cook thin slices of vegetables or meat over high heat in a small amount of oil, stirring constantly to ensure even cooking in a short time. The traditional cooking vessel is a Chinese wok; a heavy-bottomed frying pan may also be used.

Stock: a savoury liquid made by simmering aromatic vegetables, herbs and spices and usually meat, bones and trimmings in water (recipes, page 139). Stock forms a flavour-rich base for sauces.

Sugar snap peas: a variation of garden peas, introduced comparatively recently. Once stem and string are removed the entire pod may be eaten, even when fully mature.

Swede: a cruciferous root vegetable resembling a turnip but with reddish-brown skin and yellow flesh.

Sweet potato: either one of two types of nutritious tuber, one with yellowish mealy flesh, the other with a moist, sweet, orange flesh. The latter is often sold as yam but should not be confused with the true yam, see below.

Tahini (also called sesame paste): a nutty-tasting paste made from ground sesame seeds that are usually roasted.

Tarragon: a strong herb with a sweet anise taste. In combination with other herbs — especially rosemary, sage or thyme — it should be used sparingly, to avoid a clash of flavours. Because heat intensifies tarragon's flavour, cooked dishes require smaller amounts.

Thyme: a versatile herb with a zesty, slightly fruity flavour and strong aroma.

Timbale: a creamy mixture of vegetables or meat baked in a mould. The term, French for "kettledrum" also denotes a drum-shaped baking dish.

Tomato paste: a concentrated tomato purée, available in cans and tubes, used in sauces and soups. See also Puréed tomatoes.

Total fat: an individual's daily intake of polyunsaturated, monounsaturated and saturated fats. Nutritionists recommend that fats provide no more than 35 per cent of the energy in the diet. The term as used in this book refers to the combined fats in a given dish or food.

Turmeric: a spice used as a colouring agent and occasionally as a substitute for saffron. It has a musty odour and a slightly bitter flavour.

Vine leaves: the tender, lightly flavoured leaves of the grapevine, used in many ethnic cuisines as wrappers for savoury mixtures. Because the leaves are usually packed in brine, they should be rinsed before use.

Virgin olive oil: see Olive oil.

Water bath (also called bain-marie): a large pan filled part way with hot water and placed in a preheated oven as a cooking vessel for foods in smaller containers. The combination of ambient hot water and air serves to cook the food slowly and evenly.

Water chestnut: the walnut-sized tuber of an aquatic Asian plant, with rough, brown skin and white, mildly sweet, crunchy flesh.

White pepper: a powder ground from the same dried berry as that used to make black pepper, but with the berry's outer shell removed before grinding, resulting in a milder flavour. Used as a less visible alternative to black pepper in light-coloured foods.

Yam: a number of varieties of hairy tuber, rich in vitamin A and similar in taste, when cooked, to the potato. Sometimes known as the Indian potato, it should not be confused with the sweet potato, which is sometimes also sold as yam. The yam is less sweet and less widely available than the sweet potato.

Yogurt: a smooth-textured, semi-solid cultured milk product made with varying percentages of fat. Yogurt makes an excellent substitute for soured cream in cooking. Yogurt may also be combined with soured cream to produce a sauce or topping that is lower in fat and calories than soured cream alone.

Index

Picture Credits

All of the photographs in *Fresh Ways with Vegetables* were taken by staff photographer Renée Comet unless otherwise indicated below:

Cover: James Murphy. 2 top and centre: Carolyn Wall Rothery. 4: Michael Ward *(top)*, Taran Z Photography *(right)*. 5 top left: Taran Z Photography. 6: Richard Jeffery. 12: Michael Ward. 13: Taran Z Photography.

14, 15: Michael Ward. 17: Michael Latil. 18, 19, 20: Michael Ward. 22, 23: John Elliott. 44 bottom: Taran Z Photography. 47 top: Taran Z Photography. 48 Michael Latil. 49: Taran Z Photography. 50 top: Steven Biver. 51 bottom, 52: Taran Z Photography. 53: Michael Latil. 55: Michael Latil. 72 top: Taran Z Photography. 79 top: Michael Latil. 80: John Elliott. 81, 82: Michael Latil. 84: Michael Latil *(left)*, Taran Z Photography *(right)*. 88: Taran Z Photography. 93: Steven Biver. 95: Taran Z

Photography. 100, 101: Steven Biver. 103: Michael Ward. 109, 110: Taran Z Photography. 111: bottom: Taran Z Photography. 112: John Elliott. 114: Steven Biver. 115: Taran Z Photography. 116 bottom: Steven Biver. 117: Taran Z Photography. 120, 121 top: Michael Latil. 122, 123: Michael Latil. 125: Chris Knaggs. 126 bottom: Michael Latil. 129: Chris Knaggs. 130: Michael Latil. 131: Chris Knaggs. 138: Taran Z Photography.

Acknowledgements

The editors are particularly indebted to Pat Alburey, Royston, Herts., England; Nora Carey, Paris; China Closet, Bethesda, Md., U.S.A.; Chong Su Han, Grass Roots Restaurant, Alexandria, Va., U.S.A.; Jenni Fleetwood, Leiston, Suffolk, England; Kitchen Bazaar, Washington, D. C.; Brenda Tolliver, Washington, D.C.; Tina Ujlaki, New York, N.Y.; Moya de Wet, London; CiCi Williamson, Arlington, Va., U.S.A.

The editors also thank the following: Mary Jane Blandford, Alexandria, Va., U.S.A.; Dr. John Brown,

Health Education Council, London; Jackie Chalkley, Washington, D.C.; Nic Colling, Home Produce Company, Alexandria, Va., U.S.A.: Lynn Corbyn, Burgess Hill, Sussex, England; Shirley Corriher, Atlanta, Ga., U.S.A.; Carolyn Dille, Brookeville, Md., U.S.A.; Rex Downey, Oxon Hill, Md., U.S.A.; The Fresh Fruit and Vegetable Information Bureau, London; Kossow Gourmet Produce, Washington, D.C.; Dr. Luise Light, National Cancer Institute, Bethesda, Md., U.S.A.; Ruth H. Matthews, U.S. Department of Agriculture, Hyattsville, Md., U.S.A.; The National Dairy Council,

London; Lisa Ownby, Alexandria, Va., U.S.A.; Joyce Piotrowski, Vienna, Va., U.S.A.; Deborah Stapell, United Fresh Fruit and Vegetable Association, Alexandria, Va., U.S.A.; Straight from the Crate, Inc., Alexandria, Va., U.S.A.; Dr. Alley Watada, U.S. Department of Agriculture, Beltsville, Md., U.S.A.; Williams-Sonoma, Washington, D.C.

The editors wish to thank Peter Jones, Knightsbridge, London, for the loan of cutlery and tableware on pages 22, 23, 80, 129 and 131.

Typesetting by G. Beard and Son Ltd, Brighton, Sussex, England
Printed and bound by Oriental Press, Dubai